The Challenges of Uncertainty

NEW READINGS

Introductions to European Literature and Culture

CREATIVE TENSIONS:
An Introduction to Seventeenth-Century French Literature
Nicholas Hammond

"A fine feat of overall disposition ...
This impressive book should ...
provide inspiration for all of us who teach that period"

Michael Moriarty, *French Studies*

"an excellent introduction
to the period, lively, readable and scholarly"

Times Literary Supplement

FORTHCOMING:

ROMANTIC REALITIES
An Introduction to Nineteenth-Century French Literature

The Challenges of Uncertainty

An Introduction to Seventeenth-Century Spanish Literature

Jeremy Robbins

ROWMAN & LITTLEFIELD PUBLISHERS, INC.
Lanham • Boulder • New York

First published in the United States of America
in 1998 by
Rowman & Littlefield Publishers, Inc.
4720 Boston Way, Lanham, MD 20706

First published in 1998 by
Gerald Duckworth & Co. Ltd.

A catalogue record for this book is available
from the British Library.

ISBN 0-8476-9327-9 (cloth)
ISBN 0-8476-9328-7 (pbk)

Typeset by Derek Doyle & Associates
Mold, Flintshire
Printed in Great Britain by
Page Bros (Norwich) Ltd

Contents

Acknowledgments

I would like to thank a number of people and institutions: Nicholas Hammond, for his comments as editor and his encouragement as a friend; E. C. Riley, David Howarth, Eric Southworth, and Robert Pring-Mill, for stimulating conversations at various times around some of the areas dealt with here; the National Gallery, London, for permission to reproduce the self-portrait by Murillo on the cover; the Faculty Group Research Committee of the University of Edinburgh for a research award, and Jenny Lowe for her willingness to reorganize my teaching to enable me to complete the work; and lastly David Ingham, for his enthusiasm and insight. For many past and future times in Spain, this book is, as ever, for him.

Author's Note

In keeping with the format of this series, bibliographic references
have been kept to a minimum. References to Saavedra Fajardo's
Idea and Gracián's *Oráculo manual* are to essay and aphorism
number respectively, and in the case of *Don Quijote* and *El Criticón*
to book and chapter number. References to plays are by act
number alone. All translations are my own. Dates of works are normally given on their first mention only; dates for first performance
of plays are usually approximate.

Illustrations from Saavedra Fajardo's *Idea de un príncipe político-
cristiano* are taken from the first English translation (London,
1700), and are all but identical to those found in the definitive
Spanish edition of this work (Milan, 1642).

An interpretative introduction to the Baroque cannot aim to
cover in detail every aspect of the period. Inevitably some genres
and individuals receive more attention than others in so far as I
deem them more representative of cultural concerns and practices
over the whole century. The works listed at the end of each chapter
offer suggestions for further lines of enquiry; those at the end of
Chapter One also include general surveys of specific aspects of
Baroque culture – theatre, art, poetry, the picaresque etc.

Preface

The seventeenth century was the century during which Spain produced its finest and most influential works of art, poetry, prose and
drama. In this study I offer an interpretative introduction to this
period which produced some of the greatest figures of Spanish culture: the writers Cervantes, Quevedo and Gracián; the playwrights
Lope de Vega, Tirso de Molina, and Calderón de la Barca; the poet
Góngora; and the artists Velázquez and Murillo. These figures
greatly influenced contemporaries and have continued to exercise
a profound influence on modern culture: Spanish plays were
eagerly adapted by French dramatists of the stature of Molière and
Corneille; such was the prestige of Spanish prose (both fiction and
non-fiction) that it was rapidly translated into the major European
languages in the seventeenth century, with Cervantes becoming
the undisputed founder of the modern novel; over the centuries
Velázquez has exerted an enormous influence over such artists and
thinkers as Goya, Manet, Picasso and Foucault; and the poetry of
Góngora has similarly fascinated twentieth century poets, especially those of the Generation of 27 such as Federico García Lorca.

The emphasis of this study will be on the major themes, trends,
and ideas which justify viewing the century as a separate period
under the descriptive term of the Baroque. Whilst there are certainly various points of continuity between the sixteenth and the
seventeenth centuries, the seventeenth century possesses its own
distinct identity. I shall argue that this is due primarily to the fact
that seventeenth-century Spanish culture was profoundly influenced by the crisis in knowledge which was a marked feature of the

early modern period. Indeed I believe that this intellectual crisis, which can be clearly traced to the close of the sixteenth century with the burgeoning of interest in scepticism, was the most significant formative influence on the direction taken by Spanish culture during the century.

It led to what I shall call a culture of uncertainty taking hold of the artistic imagination. Intellectual uncertainties challenged many of the greatest artists and writers to explore the limits of human knowledge, and the problems and dilemmas that result from these, and in so doing to examine the complex relationship between reality and illusion, fact and fiction. This led to the creation of works of art and literature which in turn sought to challenge the viewer / reader. Such a culture of uncertainty is only exhausted in the final decades of the century as individuals pragmatically embrace the view that absolute certainty is an unobtainable ideal, and thereby move away from viewing uncertainty and doubt as intellectual obstacles. This shift in mentality signals the end of the Baroque just as definitively as the change in dynasty from the Habsburgs to the Bourbons with Charles II's death in 1700.

Together with the general culture of uncertainty, I shall consider other social and political factors which shaped the Spanish Baroque such as the resurgence of Catholic militancy and the slow decline in Spanish power. All of these compelled Spaniards to confront new or changing religious, political, and intellectual realities. The decline in political authority in particular resulted in a loss of national confidence which must be set against the parallel crisis in knowledge, for the two are obviously intimately connected. As a consequence of such a loss in confidence and certainty, the Spanish Baroque is marked by a profound sense of individuals exploring, sometimes reluctantly, sometimes enthusiastically, their rapidly changing world and the possibilities and challenges this offered.

The picture that emerges is of a culture vigorously engaged in questioning its own assumptions and beliefs, and striving to make the individual reader and spectator engage too in actively exploring and questioning his or her received ideas and ideals. This engagement of reader with text, of viewer with canvas, is what makes Baroque literature and art so vibrant. This is what gives it its characteristic sense of questioning the boundaries of behaviour, belief, and representation, and of blurring the normally clear-cut and rigidly demarcated divisions between reality and fantasy, fact and fiction. We see in such art and literature a culture provoked by change, alive to possibility, and reacting vigorously to the challenges of uncertainty.

I

Political, Intellectual, and Social Contexts

Introduction

The seventeenth century was a time of dramatic and deeply disturbing change in Europe: the centre of political power shifted away from Spain and many states became more recognizably modern as politics gradually became more secular, less dominated by religion. At the same time philosophy and science began to establish their own procedures and objectives, moving away from the preconceptions and preoccupations of Christianity and Classical authorities like Aristotle. Understandably, to live during this period was both a disturbing and an exciting experience. New intellectual ideas, and changes in political and social structures, were exhilarating and also profoundly unsettling.

In Spain, art and literature were one of the principal ways of confronting these various changes and new ideas, whether in an attempt to explore and assimilate them, or to reject and repudiate them. Consequently, to understand the themes, style and objectives of Spanish culture in this century we need to appreciate the political and intellectual factors to which Spaniards were reacting and responding, together with the social contexts in which this culture was produced and received. Such factors and contexts will be explored in this chapter not as mere background information, but rather as the very formative influences which drove Spain to create the greatest works of art, prose, theatre and poetry that it has ever produced.

For seventeenth-century Spaniards the world had become a far more ambivalent, less straightforward, place. Nothing was as it seemed. Quite literally people began to doubt the evidence of their senses. And once this process of losing confidence in the ability to interpret accurately the external world had begun, the effect was to create a view of reality as being overwhelmed with deceit and illusion. Mateo Alemán expresses this pessimistic view of the impotence of humans when faced with the manifest deceptions of the world in his picaresque novel *Guzmán de Alfarache* (Part 1 1599, Part 2 1604):

> [el engaño] es una red sutilísima . . . Es tan imperceptible y delgada, que no hay tan clara vista, juicio tan sutil ni discreción tan limada, que pueda descubrirla; . . . Es tan general esta contagiosa enfermedad, que no solamente los hombres la padecen, mas las aves y animales. . . . El tiempo, las ocasiones, los sentidos nos engañan. Y sobre todo, aun los más bien trazados pensamientos. Toda cosa engaña. (*Guzmán de Alfarache*, II.1.3)

> ([Deceit] is a very fine net . . . It is so imperceptible and thin that it cannot be discovered by the most penetrating eyes, the subtlest mind, or the most finely honed intelligence; . . . This contagious disease is so widespread that not only do men suffer from it, but the birds and animals as well. . . . Everything deceives us, time, events, feelings, even the most carefully planned thoughts. Everything deceives.)

Deceit (*engaño*) was one of the obsessions of the period: how to detect it, how to avoid it, and even how to exploit it. Viewing the world as one of deceit led in turn to a profound sense of universal distrust in surface appearances (*parecer*). The deeply pessimistic misogynist Francisco de Quevedo, for example, frequently depicts the world as 'al revés' (up-side down) – doctors are murderers, the devout are hypocrites, and beautiful women are in reality little better than whores. Provoked and challenged by the world around them, writers and artists produced work which in turn provokes and challenges. Baroque artists sought above all to incite a reac-

tion on the level of both the senses and the mind, and they
employed a variety of means to do this, including the use of complex imagery, difficult syntax, shocking and violent subject matter,
and striking juxtapositions of antithetical concepts (life / death,
body / soul, heaven / earth).

One of the driving forces behind this desire to provoke was to
force the individual to question his or her assumptions and priorities, and to correct and realign them if necessary. This led to
starkly pessimistic statements designed to shake us out of our com-
placency, as when Rodrigo Méndez Silva writes 'no es esta vida más
que una figura de vida, y una sombra de la muerte . . . ayer estabas
vivo, y hoy estás muerto en la sepultura, y desengáñate, que en el
instante que naciste, comenzaste a morir' (*Engaños y desengaños del
mundo* [1655]: 'this life is nothing more than a simulacrum of life,
a reflection of death . . . yesterday you were alive, today you lie
dead in your grave; wake up and see the truth, for as soon as you
were born, you started to die').

In one sense, then, Baroque culture is profoundly moralistic.
However, such moralism is not always necessarily Christian in
nature or purpose, nor does it preclude enjoyment and entertainment in the work of art. Indeed, this desire to provoke actually
tends to make Baroque art and literature extremely sensual and
voluptuous, precisely because it was felt that to arouse the senses
was the first step in stimulating the mind. Like the Renaissance,
then, the Baroque followed the dictum of the Latin poet Horace
that art should both please and instruct, but unlike the
Renaissance, the instruction more often than not consisted in provoking questions rather than providing answers. It is the main
argument of this book in fact that Baroque culture was above all
else a culture of challenges and questions rather than one of set-
tled assumptions and established answers. Nowhere is such urgent
questioning more prevalent than in Spain.

Before looking at how artists and writers expressed and
explored the ambivalence, pessimism and questioning spirit of
their society – the subject of the rest of this study – we need to

explore the factors which were instrumental in making Spaniards
feel so ambivalent about themselves and the world around them.
It is possible to identify several factors intimately connected with
the political, intellectual and social contexts of seventeenth-century culture which contributed to the mentality I have just been
describing. I propose to focus on four of these: (1) the Spanish
political situation, both nationally and internationally; (2) the
influence of religion and the Catholic Reformation; (3) the impact
of Classical philosophy; and (4) the influence of the physical set-
tings and circumstances in which much Baroque art and literature
was encountered.

1. The Spanish Decline

It was a fact recognized by Spaniards themselves that over the seventeenth century the balance of power in Europe shifted
inexorably from Spain to France. On the most basic of levels
Spaniards had to watch as their world empire, formed over the
course of the previous century, was threatened and eroded by
other European powers. It has been convincingly argued that
Spain's political fortune declined primarily because, becoming
involved in the horrific pan-European Thirty Years War (1618-48),
it attempted to wage war on so many fronts and, inevitably, lacked
the resources to do so successfully. In the 1640s, for example,
Spain was actively at war with the Dutch Republic and France, was
committed to supporting various theatres of war in the Habsburg
Holy Roman Empire, and had to contend with two revolts within
the peninsula itself when both Portugal and Catalonia rebelled
against Habsburg rule in 1640. The Thirty Years War was one of the
bloodiest fought until that date in Europe. The Spanish diplomat
Diego de Saavedra Fajardo who had first-hand experience of Italy
and Germany writes of the atrocities, bloodshed, destruction and
devastation that this long war brought to Europe. Understandably
such experiences imbued many Europeans with a sense of despair
and pessimism.

Desengaño = disillusion
engaño = deceit

In Spain the drain on human and financial resources and the perception of almost inevitable defeat and loss of public reputation led to a type of disillusionment which is one of the main features of Spanish culture of this period. *Desengaño*, to give it its Spanish name, typifies Spanish Baroque culture. The English term 'disillusion' barely even suggests the nuances of the Spanish term which conveys the notion of the profound, almost existential, realization of the absolute vanity of human values and possessions, together with a realignment of priorities in the light of such a realization.

Desengaño appears in both religious and secular contexts. It always implies a moral stance of detachment and distance, not necessarily a desire to withdraw from the world, but rather a desire to view it in the correct perspective. This aspect of *desengaño* is encapsulated by the Portuguese Antonio López de Vega who sets out his philosophy to the *sabio* (wise man) as follows: 'el desengaño de las imperfecciones del mundo y de las calamidades de la humana vida le debe tener armado y prevenido al sabio, para que ningún suceso le hiera con sobresalto y fuerza de repentino' (*Heráclito y Demócrito de nuestro siglo* [1641]: 'Disillusion with the imperfections of the world and the disasters of human life must strengthen and prepare the wise man so that nothing will strike him suddenly and unawares').

Many contemporaries viewed the decline of Spain as something inevitable and natural, if lamentable. Saavedra encapsulated this viewpoint in his *empresa* (a pictorial device which carries symbolic meaning) depicting an arrow, with the motto 'O subir o bajar' ('Either up or down'), explaining his thoughts in the ensuing essay as follows: 'Lo que más sube, más cerca está de su caída. En llegando las cosas a su último estado, han de volver a bajar sin detenerse' (*Idea de un príncipe político-cristiano* [1640 / 1642], 60: 'What goes up furthest is nearest to its fall. As soon as things reach their highest point, they immediately start to fall').

This view of events having their own momentum tended to make Spaniards at the time cling to concepts such as constancy (holding firm in the face of adversity) and prudence (the ability to scrutinize past events and present circumstances to enable the correct course of future actions to be chosen). These two terms became the key concepts of Spanish statecraft, with Saavedra depicting them as being locked in a relationship of interdependence, the one compensating for the inevitable limitations of the other: 'así como es oficio de la prudencia el prevenir, lo es de la fortaleza y constancia el tolerar lo que no pudo huir la prudencia' (*Idea*, 37: 'just as it is the role of prudence to foresee, so it is the role of fortitude and constancy to endure what prudence could not flee'). Constancy and prudence formed an essential part of Neostoicism, the Christianized version of Stoicism revived by the Flemish Justus Lipsius at the close of the sixteenth century. It stressed the importance of inner tranquillity in the face of events beyond one's control and gave Europeans a philosophy to adhere to during the bitter and bloody religious wars in the first half of the century.

This Neostoic attitude was not one of passivity but rather of resignation in the face of circumstances and events beyond an individual's control. The key religious debates of the period over free will and predestination were similarly concerned with the scope and limitations of human agency. Consequently many of the greatest works written during the century explore the causes and the consequences of the limitations of an individual to shape or be shaped by his / her environment. Miguel de Cervantes' *Don Quijote de la Mancha* (1605 and 1615) depicts the deranged hero attempting to shape events and reinterpret and order the world, only to fail spectacularly; Pedro Calderón de la Barca's *La vida es sueño* (c1630) traces the personal and social education of a prince imprisoned since birth in an isolated tower by his own father, who feels that his son is destined to overthrow him, as he questions, rebels against, and eventually accepts the limitations set by society on human freedom; while Tirso de Molina's play *El condenado por desconfiado* (1621-5) dramatizes the hermit Paulo's despair and downfall brought about by his too rigid belief in God's predestination and his refusal to exercise free will positively.

In the political sphere many writers treat the same questions of freedom and the ability to control and shape events at national and international levels, whether from a rabidly anti-Machiavellian stance, like the Jesuit Pedro de Ribadeneira (*Tratado de la religión y virtudes* [1595]), or from a more pragmatic position, often heavily influenced by the writings of the Roman historian Tacitus, like Baltasar Alamos de Barrientos (*Tácito español* [1614]), Joaquín Setanti (*Centellas de varios conceptos* [1614]), Baltasar Gracián (*El político don Fernando el Católico* [1640]), and Saavedra (*Idea de un príncipe político-cristiano*). Whilst some of these literary and political works are pessimistic and some optimistic, all basically accept the notion that the individual is limited in what he or she can do, and seek to explore how we might come to accept this and to what extent we can overcome the problems that this causes.

It is easy to exaggerate the effects of the loss of power and hence prestige on Spain. After all, Spain was not defeated easily: war with France lasted some 24 years (1635-59) before ending in the Treaty of the Pyrenees, favourable to the French. Spain's decline was not rapid. This said, the effect of this inexorable decline can be dramatically conveyed by considering the reduction in Spanish territory by the end of the Spanish War of Succession in 1713, a war occasioned by the death of the last Spanish Habsburg king, Charles II, without an heir. Over the course of the century Spain had lost the Dutch Republic (1648), Portugal (1668), Franche-Comté (1678), and, between 1713-14, the Spanish Netherlands, Naples, Milan, Sicily, Sardinia, Minorca and Gibraltar. The paradox is that it was against this backdrop of slow decline that the magnificent cultural achievements of the Spanish Baroque flourished.

2. The Catholic Reformation

Typically *desengaño* finds expression through two ubiquitous terms, appearance (*parecer*) and reality (*ser*), with most writers and indeed artists suggesting that the only true reality is found in heaven, since everything on earth is merely a transient, pale copy of this more lasting reality. Such a perception of the greater reality of heaven leads us to the second major factor influencing the Spanish Baroque, the impact on society of the Catholic Reformation. After the spread of Protestantism in the sixteenth century, the Catholic Church decided to seize the initiative in a counter-offensive intended to win back the hearts and minds of individuals to Catholicism. The first step was taken when Catholic dogma was carefully defined and affirmed during the twenty-five sessions of the Council of Trent (1545-1563).

This resurgence of militancy and confidence also led to the establishment of new religious orders. Preeminent amongst these was the Society of Jesus, the Jesuits, founded in 1540 by the Spaniard St Ignatius of Loyola, who spearheaded this Catholic offensive. Many writers were influenced by the Jesuits since many were educated in their schools, including Calderón and Quevedo, and many Jesuits themselves were active intellectuals engaged in theological, spritual, philosophical, political and literary activities. The Jesuit Baltasar Gracián, for example, engaged in all these activities in print, with the exception of the first.

In its final session the Council of Trent recommended the deployment of art as a means of revitalising faith, reasoning that

> by means of the histories of our redemption, portrayed by paintings or other representations, the people are instructed, and confirmed in the habit of remembering, and continually revolving in their minds the articles of faith; as also that great profit is derived from all sacred images ... because the miracles which God has performed by means of the saints, and their salutary examples, are set before the eyes of the faithful.

As a direct result of this the Church began to employ art in an attempt to captivate people's imaginations and so stimulate their faith. This led to the development of a style of religious art which was designed to arouse the senses of the spectator and so lead to an intense affirmation of the truths of Catholic dogma. This use of art will be considered in detail in Chapter Four.

Devotional art and literature increased greatly over this period as a consequence, and artistic subjects were often chosen so as to affirm the centrality of distinctive features of Catholicism criticised and rejected by Protestants: the monastic orders, the Virgin Mary, transubstantiation (the belief that the consecrated bread and wine change into the body and blood of Christ), and the martyrdom of Saints whose deaths were conceived as an example to the faithful and a reaffirmation of the true Church's history. Part of the impact of this deployment of art was that it served to emphasize the centrality of religion in people's lives. This served in turn to reinforce the importance of viewing thoughts and actions from the perspective of eternity, rather than simply from a transient human perspective.

3. The Impact of Classical Philosophy

The third area of influence is one which I shall emphasize heavily over the course of the subsequent chapters, since it has received little attention in comparison with the questions of national crisis and Catholic militancy. Part of the Humanistic legacy of the Renaissance was the rediscovery of Classical literature and thought. Two types of ancient philosophical schools radically shaped the Baroque mind, moving it towards a more recognizably modern outlook. These were Stoicism and scepticism. I have already mentioned Neostoicism and its impact, and its central notions are usefully summarized by Quevedo, who as a young man had communicated with Justus Lipsius, and who was one of Spain's leading advocates of the benefits of a philosophy which would help one accept the limitations of the human condition:

> La doctrina toda de los estoicos se cierra en este principio: que las cosas se dividen en propias y ajenas; que las propias están en nuestra mano, y las ajenas en la mano ajena; que aquéllas nos tocan, que estotras no nos pertenecen, y que por esto no nos han de perturbar ni afligir; que no hemos de procurar que en las cosas se haga nue-

stro deseo, sino ajustar nuestro deseo con los sucesos de las cosas; que así tendremos libertad, paz y quietud, y al contrario siempre andaremos quejosos y turbados. (*Nombre, origen, intento, recomendación y descendencia de la doctrina estoica* [1635])

(The whole doctrine of the Stoics is encapsulated in this one principle: things can be divided into 'internals' and 'externals'; the former fall within our own control and therefore concern us, the latter beyond our control and thus our concern, to the extent that they should neither disturb nor bother us. We must not seek to make things conform to our own desires, but rather make our desires conform to how things actually are. In this way we will obtain freedom, peace and calm, and if we don't do this we will in contrast always be discontented and perturbed.)

The Stoics' emphasis on a clear division between what we can and cannot influence is consonant with the realignment of perspective at the heart of *desengaño*, and indicates how much the notion of *desengaño* owed to the ethical doctrines of Neostoicism.

Scepticism in contrast teaches that all claims to human knowledge are false. The basis for this belief was that, since our entire knowledge of the external world is based on sense-information, and since our senses are patently capable of being deceived, we can never be certain that such information is true.

A classic example cited by many seventeenth-century writers of how our senses deceive us is that the sun appears to us to be a very small disc, whereas we know from mathematics that it is in fact a much bigger object. This example encapsulates the disjunction between appearance and reality that obsessed Spanish thought. As Baltasar Gracián writes in one of his aphorisms headed *Realidad y apariencia,* 'Las cosas no pasan por lo que son, sino por lo que parecen' (*Oráculo manual y arte de prudencia* [1647], 99: 'Things are not taken for what they are, but for what they appear to be').

Saavedra illustrates this with a picture of a shell containing a pearl (see illustration 1), on which example he comments:

Illustration 1

Diego de Saavedra Fajardo, *Idea de un príncipe político-cristiano*
(Empresa 32)

Concibe la concha del rocío del cielo, y en lo cándido de sus
entrañas crece y se descubre aquel puro parto de la perla. Nadie juz-
garía su belleza por lo exterior tosco y mal pulido. Así se engañan
los sentidos en el examen de las acciones exteriores, obrando por
las primeras apariencias de las cosas, sin penetrar lo que está dentro
de ellas. (32)

(The oyster conceives from the dew of heaven and in its pure white
innards the perfect pearl grows. Nobody would judge its beauty
from such a coarse and rough exterior. In this way our senses are
deceived when they consider external actions, working from the
first impressions of things without delving to discover what is
beneath them.)

The impact of scepticism on Spain has been largely ignored, yet it
plays a formative role in key works such as Cervantes' *Don Quijote
de la Mancha* and Gracián's *El Criticón* (Part 1 1651, Part 2 1653,
Part 3 1657), as we shall see in Chapters Two and Three.
Furthermore, it encouraged Spaniards to view reality in terms of
the antithesis between *ser* and *parecer*, and in so doing stimulated
people to adopt a more critical and questioning attitude towards
received opinion and in turn towards the prevailing world view.

The questioning mentality encouraged – indeed demanded –
by scepticism revolutionized the ways in which reality was concep-
tualized. In Europe this led to the work of individuals like René
Descartes and Isaac Newton which transformed philosophy and
science and created a more secular world in which science
replaced faith as the arbiter of reality. Dogma and certainty were
gradually replaced by probability and a new flexibility regarding
the provisional nature of human knowledge.

Spain produced no figure of the stature of Descartes or Newton,
but this in no way justifies the caricature of Spain as a backward and
repressive regime. It is all too convenient to forget the struggles
which most innovators encountered in England, France and Italy in
the pursuit and propagation of their views, and the longevity of the
Classical and Medieval world views which they were eventually to

displace totally. Moreover, there is much evidence that Spaniards were well aware of innovations elsewhere in Europe.

By the second half of the century many writers show an awareness of the sceptical trends of European thought, with attitudes ranging from that of Antonio López de Vega who advocates an outlook premised on the provisional nature of all human knowledge – he goes as far as to advocate premising most of our statements with 'parece ...' ('it seems ...') rather than with 'es ...' ('it is ...') (*Heráclito y Demócrito*); to Francisco Gutiérrez de los Ríos who recommends pragmatism and utility as the sole means of deciding not only on a particular course of action, but also on which philosophy to adopt as one's own (*El hombre práctico* [1686]).

They are also clearly familiar with the ideas of major European thinkers. References to Descartes and his writings, for example, can be found in both vernacular and Latin texts, while other figures closely associated with scepticism, such as the ancient philosopher Carneades who first developed the idea of probability as the basis for deciding a course of action in the absence of any clear truth, exert a profound influence on writers such as Gracián and Calderón. Where Spanish thought has its greatest contact with European trends is in its similar preoccupations: the nature of reality and illusion, the fallibility of the senses, the limitations of reason and the all-pervasive fascination with perception.

The obsession with perception is also a result of the new cosmology, the scientific verification that the earth was not the centre of creation but did, in fact, revolve around the sun. The conflict between the geocentric (earth-centred) and the heliocentric (sun-centred) model of the heavens made people question their position in the world and forced them to confront the absolute relativity of any one individual's viewpoint. In this way absolutism gave way to relativism, the particular instance gained ground over the universal cause or explanation.

The question of perception was also intimately linked with that of deception: can we trust our senses and the information they provide, given that we know they do on occasions fool us? From this speculation it was a short step to broader questions such as what is the exact status of our knowledge of the external world? Can it ever be secure and true, or is it always bound to be provisional given the limitations of our human perspective and the fallibility of our senses? Perceptual issues raised deeply provocative and alarming philosophical questions.

4. The Performative Contexts of Baroque Culture

The social context in which a work of art, a play or indeed a piece of literature was encountered exercised a decisive influence on its style and content. In turn, the context operated as a powerful force in shaping exactly how art and literature were understood and interpreted. A consideration of the occasions for which art and literature were produced serves to emphasize the social diversity and the gendering of the cultural experience. As we shall see, access to culture differed from one sphere of cultural production or activity to another, with questions of class and gender playing a decisive element in defining both access and participation. Furthermore, a consideration of the places in which Baroque culture was encountered will offset the view which I have so far given of that culture being pessimistic, serious and conflictive. There is another side to the Baroque which, while it also explored these darker themes and sentiments, was extremely playful, mesmerising and expressive. To ignore this aspect is to misrepresent the diversity and complexity which makes the art and literature of this period so dynamic and arresting.

(a) The Court

When the young Philip IV ascended the throne in 1621 only days before his sixteenth birthday, the Count-Duke of Olivares, his mentor and eventual favourite, consciously set about educating the king and creating a dazzling court worthy of such a powerful monarch. The effects of this programme ranged from the creation of a new 'pleasure palace', the Buen Retiro in Madrid which had its own theatre, ballroom, galleries, bullring, gardens, and artificial lakes, to the employment of the greatest artists, dramatists and poets to sing the praises and record the deeds of the king and his court. The Court thus became the major source of secular patronage, and artists and writers flocked to Madrid from all over Spain in pursuit of patronage.

Often their hopes and ambitions were never realized, so fuelling the sense of *desengaño* prevalent already in seventeenth-century culture. However some individuals like the dramatist Calderón de la Barca and the painter Diego de Velázquez gained greatly from royal patronage and they in turn moulded an image of the king and helped create the illusion of power and authority – a form of propaganda – necessary to sustain the image of Philip IV, the Planet King, so called as the sun was believed to be the fourth planet in the heavens. (Philip's nephew, Louis XIV of France, more famously called the Sun King, learnt much from his uncle's manipulation of images and symbols.)

The Court's patronage affected one area above all others – the theatre. Court drama aimed to create a perfect illusion and to this end employed some of the greatest playwrights, artists and stage designers of the day. Unlike commercial theatre, it employed perspective scenery, a relatively new Italian invention, so that the stage took on the realistic appearance of the location of the play. Stage machinery was employed to further the illusion and astound the audience: gods and goddesses flew through the air, ships appeared amidst waves, mountains turned into palaces, forests into ornamental gardens. If such innovatory techniques appealed to the eye, then music was employed to delight the ear. The use of recitation led to short plays being entirely sung, the forerunner of the Spanish *zarzuela*. Court theatre, taking as its subjects tales from Classical mythology, epitomizes how Baroque art aimed to delight the senses. Productions were understandably expensive, and were occasions when the theatricality of the court with its elaborate protocol was brought face to face with theatre proper, the illusion created by one matching the illusion created by the other.

Such spectacles have long been regarded as essentially frivolous and lacking in artistic merit, and the king was often heavily criticized for his devotion to them: one preacher, arriving soaked to deliver a sermon to Philip IV, declared bluntly that '¡Para un predicador de Vuestra Majestad falta un coche en un día como éste, y sobran tantos en que vengan a festejarle representantes!' ('On a day like this there is not a coach to spare for Your Majesty's preacher, yet there are always plenty to bring actors to entertain you!'). Such criticisms failed to appreciate the political dimensions of these dramatic spectacles. These were occasions when the king could project an image of cultured refinement and prodigious wealth to visiting dignitaries, a necessary part of statecraft at the time. Indeed illustrated manuscripts describing these events were sent to the Habsburg Court in Vienna and so broadcast Spain's cultural pretensions further afield.

Moreover, some of the court dramas produced by Calderón are powerful pieces full of beautiful poetry, and the subject matter was often chosen to reflect contemporary events or give a polite lesson to King and court alike. Many plays, for example, like Calderón's *El mayor encanto, amor* (1635), *Los tres mayores prodigios* (1636) and *El monstruo de los jardines* (1660s), depict palace life as effeminate and negative, serving to remind the royal spectator that duty should come before pleasure, government before entertainment. Warning the court against court life as the court sits in splendid array in a palace theatre may seem somewhat paradoxical, yet the lesson was a pertinent one for a king like Philip IV who was renowned for his love of theatre (and actresses). This belief in the emasculating effects of the court was something of a constant in political writing, being repeatedly mentioned by Saavedra in his *Idea*.

(b) The Church

For all the artistic importance of the Court, the major source of commissions for most artists throughout the century was the

Church. If access to Court art was restricted, Church art was accessible to all, and even the poorest could view and enjoy the work of Spain's greatest artists. Artists were given precise instructions by those commissioning work as to the iconographical content of their work: Velázquez's father-in-law, Francisco Pacheco, appended a lengthy section to his *Arte de la pintura* (1649) detailing how certain religious subjects had to be portrayed to conform to Church teaching and decorum. Despite such limitations Church commissions were eagerly sought as they frequently meant secure and prestigious work producing whole cycles of paintings, such as those still *in situ* in the monastery at Guadalupe painted by Francisco de Zurbarán.

As the century progressed, decorative schemes for churches became increasingly theatrical in conception and effect. Paintings, sculpture (angels, cherubs, billowing stone clouds, twisting columns), banks of candles, incense, music: all combined to create overwhelming environments in which the individual could be transported from mundane reality. Many examples of such Baroque ornamentation still exist in Spain and Latin America.

Some of the most extravagant and lavish schemes were to be found in Seville. The Church of the Hospital de la Santa Caridad, for example, has a decorative scheme designed to challenge and comfort the individual which was created by the combined talents of two of the greatest painters, Bartolomé Esteban Murillo and Juan de Valdés Leal, as well as that of one of the greatest sculptors, Pedro Roldán, who followed the instructions of the Brotherhood's dynamic leader, Miguel de Mañara (whose wild youth led him to be identified as the prototype for Tirso de Molina's Don Juan in *El burlador de Sevilla*).

As you enter the church (it is still open to the public, though several of the canvases by Murillo which were stolen by the French at the start of the nineteenth century are missing), you are confronted by two stark canvases by Valdés Leal. These are amongst the most famous Spanish paintings of the Baroque. One depicts death as a skeleton carrying a coffin and trampling on objects of worldly value while leering out at us (*In Ictu Oculi*), while the other shows a crypt in which we see the open coffins of a bishop and a gentleman, their decaying bodies crawling with insects (*Finis Gloriae Mundi*). These two canvases are painted so graphically that they still have the potential to horrify the modern visitor. After this striking lesson as to the worthlessness of everything human and the unavoidable fact of death, we move through the church past the calmer, more comforting canvases by Murillo, which show the acts of charity and mercy which the members of the brotherhood exist to carry out, until we stand in front of the enormous altarpiece which, in three dimensions, shows the burial of Christ.

Art was commonly used to emphasize dramatically the separation of the terrestrial from the heavenly realm, as with Valdés Leal's canvases just mentioned. More dramatic still was pulpit oratory, with many sermons judged as much for their rhetorical effect as their doctrinal content. The stylistic revolution set in motion by the poet Luis de Góngora – who employed elaborate metaphors, complex syntax, recherché and Latinate vocabulary to produce a beautiful but extremely difficult style known as *culteranismo* (to be considered in Chapter Five) – was taken up in pulpits by Court preachers such as Fray Hortensio Paravicino. For modern students of the period it is easy to overlook the importance of sermons, yet the effect of Paravicino's rhetorical novelty was to arouse precisely the sense of surprise and wonder so sought after by Baroque artists and writers. Paravicino himself goes so far as to represent himself as the literary equivalent of Columbus, discovering new literary territories (*Panegírico funeral a la reina Doña Margarita de Austria* [1628]). The importance of such 'discoveries' were that the Church made them accessible to all.

(c) The Literary Academies

Unlike the *Académie française*, founded in Paris under the patrónage of Louis XIII and his first minister Richelieu, literary academies in Spain were not state-controlled, and endorsing, insti-

tutions. They were literary salons, held often in the house of a
noble patron, which provided an entertaining environment in
which writers and nobles could meet, allowing the nobles to gain
the veneer of culture and sophistication that poetry conferred, and
poets the opportunity of making contacts and gaining a literary
reputation. Both Philip IV and the Count-Duke of Olivares
attended academies in Madrid where the most illustrious groups
inevitably met. However, academies were held in all the major
Spanish towns throughout the century, with particularly influential
groups meeting in Zaragoza, Valencia and Seville.

A light humorous atmosphere prevailed, with poems submitted
on set topics, often extremely salacious, ridiculous, or dramatic in
nature: 'On a jealous man who, having made a hole in a wall to spy
on his wife, is blinded when a chunk of it gets in his eyes'; 'On a
groom who was so absent-minded that he forgot to sleep with his
bride on their wedding night'; 'On a lady losing her glass eye'.
Playfulness was quite consciously demanded of poets, with many
academies setting deliberately challenging topics to test the poets'
ingenuity, such as requiring the poem to be written entirely using
questions and exclamations, or only using words as rhymes which
were stressed on the third to last syllable (such as 'cándido',
'white').

The quality of much of this poetry is poor, but its influence was
significant. Not only did poets of the calibre of Quevedo, Góngora
and Lope de Vega attend, but the academy style – light-hearted,
ingenious, with great emphasis on word-play and far-fetched analogies – was instrumental in fostering and disseminating a taste for
wit (*agudeza*). In particular, academy topics and the way they were
treated laid great emphasis on the particular (the everyday realm
of the lovers) rather than on the universal (the abstract world of
idealized sentiments and Platonic aspirations) which had typified
Renaissance poetry. In moving in the direction of the mundane
and the circumstantial, poetry parallels the broader intellectual
trend mentioned above which set great store on effects rather than
causes, on accurate, minute descriptions of natural phenomena,

rather than on grand theories and preestablished principles. Just as the newly invented microscope drew attention to the existence of another level of reality in all its minutiae, so poetry in turn emphasized the specific and the quotidian.

(d) The Convent

The role of women was much restricted in seventeenth-century Spain. Although they attended literary academies, they never exercised the degree of patronage and hence control over these institutions which occurred in the French *salons*. The only independent space for women was the convent. Whilst many noble women entered religious orders in pursuit of religious vocations, equal numbers were required to enter by force of circumstances, if, for example, their male relatives were unable or unwilling to provide them with the dowries necessary for marriage.

It is easy to over-idealize such spaces, for the freedoms they offered were always circumscribed by male clerics who exercised ultimate authority over them. Individuals such as Sor María de Agreda, the mother superior of a convent in Aragon who carried on an intimate epistolary relationship with Philip IV over a sustained period of time and who used her letters to advise the king on matters of policy and war as well as to console him over the deaths of his children etc., are few and far between.

Nonetheless, convents offered women – above all noble women – an opportunity to pursue intellectual and literary pursuits normally closed to them in secular life. A feminist writer like María de Zayas is emphatic on this point. At the close of her collection of short stories, *Parte segunda del sarao y entretenimiento honesto* (1647), popularly known as the *Desengaños amorosos*, several of the women narrators opt to enter a convent, having been totally disillusioned by their patriarchal society, after listening to graphic stories of women being raped, tortured, murdered and physically and mentally abused by men, often their husbands, fathers and brothers. That the central character Lisis enters the convent out of a desire

for safety and freedom rather than because of a vocation is seen by
the fact that she chooses not to take full vows like her former slave,
Isabel. As Lisis explains to her betrothed:

> Y como en el juego, que mejor juzga quien mira que quien juega, yo
> viendo, no sólo en estos desengaños, mas en lo que todas las casadas
> me dan, unas lamentándose de que tienen los maridos jugadores;
> otras, amancebados, y muchas de que no atienden a su honor ...
> estoy tan cobarde, que, como el que ha cometido algún delito, me
> acojo a sagrado y tomo por amparo el retiro de un convento ... me
> voy a salvar de los engaños de los hombres. (Story 10)

> (Just as in a game the best judge is the person who doesn't take part,
> so, having seen from these stories of disenchantment and from
> real examples offered by all married women, some women
> bemoaning the fact that their husbands are gamblers, others that
> they are unfaithful, and many more that they don't take care of
> their honour ... I feel such a coward that, like a person who has
> committed a crime, I am going to seek the protection of a sanctuary
> by taking refuge in a convent ... I am going off to save myself from
> men's deceptions.)

In a sense, Lisis opts for one kind of passivity and restriction over
another, yet in so doing she unequivocally refuses to take part in
life's unequal game whose rules are all in men's favour.

The opportunities and limitations of convent life can be seen in
the life of Sor Juana Inés de la Cruz who, in her convent in Mexico,
wrote plays, as well as poetry which equals that by her greatest pre-
cursor, Góngora. She was frequently visited by the viceroy's wife (to
whom she wrote passionate love poems), and studied philosophy,
theology and science. In her *Respuesta a Sor Fileta* (written 1691),
the first consciously feminist tract in any European language,
written to counter accusations that women, and especially nuns,
should not pursue knowledge, she presents herself as insatiable for
knowledge, using even her domestic surroundings as the starting
points for intellectual inquiry.

It seems tempting now to dismiss such intellectual speculations as insignificant, but it is worthwhile noting that Sor Juana was held up as a practitioner of a view of science based on observation rather than preestablished rules at the start of the eighteenth century as some Spaniards struggled to get their country to adopt new scientific methods. This said, the attacks on Sor Juana, and her eventual 'voluntary' silencing, indicate the limitations on women even in such potentially empowering environments. Convents offered many opportunities, but these were always under threat from male-dominated society.

Conclusion

Several points emerge concerning the context in which Baroque culture was created and received:

(1) Contrary to the influential view put forward by the critic José Maravall, the Spanish Baroque was not a monolithic enterprise used to further the interests of the ruling elite. Elite it certainly could be, but never as state-controlled as French classical culture. Thus academies could become focal points for regional diversity: in Valencia, for example, academies were consciously used to resist the cultural monopoly of Madrid-based culture.

Obviously Baroque art and literature were rarely genuinely subversive of received values, but this should not lead us into thinking that they were uncritical or that voices of criticism were never able to be heard. Many writers were frankly outspoken about rule-by-favourite, running the risk thereby of alienating the most powerful man in the kingdom, the Count-Duke of Olivares. Others used indirect means of offering a sharp critique of the king's behaviour: Lope de Vega's powerful revenge tragedy, *El castigo sin venganza* (1632), opens by depicting a dissolute ruler, the Duke of Ferrara, out *incognito* searching for prostitutes, behaviour which was widely believed to mirror Philip IV's who, it was said, used to slip out of the palace with the Count-Duke in disguise in pursuit of sexual adventures. The criticism is made all the blunter when one prostitute, refusing to believe the Duke is actually present, lectures him indirectly on the unsuitability of such behaviour for a man whose future bride is arriving the following day.

Some genres actually sanctioned criticism, and thus court preachers not infrequently lectured the king on his behaviour and policies, one declaring somewhat melodramatically at the end of a sermon delivered in 1657 – exemplfying thus the theatrical nature of pulpit oratory, 'Préndanme; córtenme la cabeza, que yo cumplo con mi oficio y he de decir la verdad'! ('Arrest me! Cut off my head! I am only fulfilling my duty and speaking the truth!').

(2) Whilst access to Baroque culture was often a matter of social status, the Church enabled all manner of people to experience the impact of a style which was designed to appeal to the senses and the mind in equal measure. Furthermore commercial theatre, perhaps the most popular art form throughout the century, was also easily accessible, and the annual Corpus Christi plays, the *autos sacramentales*, were open-air performances using almost as much stage machinery etc. as court drama. Even court drama was not closed to the public. Whilst they may not have seen the opening performances and so would have missed the bizarre juxtaposition of court and theatre, the royal theatre was subsequently opened to the public to recoup the immense cost of the productions: writing in 1652 one of the many news chroniclers noted that Calderón's *La fiera, y la piedra el rayo* was seen on the first day by the royal family, on the second and third by the royal and town councils, and for thirty-seven days afterwards by the public.

(3) The role of women within this culture – as both consumers and producers – was limited. I have argued that the convent offered a degree of intellectual activity unusual for the period. Out of the convent, the participation of women within their culture varied. As consumers, women had nearly as many opportunities as men – money, class and education permitting. Women went to the theatre (though their presence there caused moralists many an

anxious moment), to church, and to literary academies, and could also obviously buy books and appreciate art.

As producers, their participation was greatly restricted by their gender. Since artistic training required being apprenticed to a painter, this meant that painting and sculpture were activities effectively closed to women: the only woman to make a name artistically was Luisa Roldán, known as La Roldana, who had the advantage of being the daughter of a famous sculptor, Pedro Roldán, who was prepared to train her.

Women fared slightly better in the field of literature. They regularly attended academies, and a variety of novels such as Alonso de Castillo Solórzano's *Las harpías en Madrid* (1631), Gabriel de Corral's *La Cintia de Aranjuez* (1629), and Luis Vélez de Guevara's *El diablo cojuelo* (1641), whose authors attended prominent academies in Madrid, depict such meetings and show the women participants as active as the men in singing and reading their verse. Indeed Zayas' two collections of short stories, the *Novelas amorosas* (1637) and the *Desengaños amorosos*, have as their frame narratives the gathering of various men and women in private to narrate the stories to one another.

This active participation is not reflected in publication however. Very rarely did a woman have her poetry included in the published accounts of academies, and when they did this was often under a pseudonym consisting merely of a Christian name. This hints at a possible reason why women found it difficult to get their works into print, namely that to publish was considered indecorous for a noble woman. Consequently, while there is plenty of evidence that women wrote fiction, autobiography, verse and drama these circulated only in manuscript. Whilst this certainly restricted the number of readers, it should be remembered that manuscript culture ran parallel with print culture during the early modern period and was an important means of transmitting ideas and literary works. This said, as the century progressed and earlier prejudices concerning the ignoble pursuit of fame via the printed word disappeared for men, very few women had their works printed. Those women who did make it into print were, for all the quality of their work, patronized by the male literary establishment as exceptions: Sor Juana, one of the century's greatest poets and its most original feminist thinker, was referred to as the Tenth Muse, a phrase which praises her while also highlighting the novelty of a female writer by presenting her as unique.

The period's misogyny as seen in writers like Quevedo and Gracián is both intense and aggressive, and women are consistently presented as incapable of the intellectual achievements and refinements of men. Thus Gracián explicitly excludes women from the projected readership of the aphorisms in his *Oráculo manual* by positing his ideal reader as unambiguously masculine, a 'varón desengañado' (100: 'disillusioned man'). Zayas explores this attitude in her stories, having one narrator suggest that men turn women into intellectual eunuchs through fear of their real capabilities:

> los hombres de temor y envidia las privan de las letras y las armas, como hacen los moros a los cristianos que han de servir donde hay mujeres, que los hacen eunucos por estar seguros de ellos. (Story 4)

> (Through fear and envy men deprive women of arms and letters, just like the Moors do to Christians who are to serve where there are women, turning them into eunuchs so that they can be more confident of them.)

In this analogy, Zayas presents knowledge as unequivocally equated with masculinity, and thereby points to the gendering of knowledge within the period.

(4) Baroque culture is striking for the degree to which it was experienced communally: theatre, academies, churches, all provided public space for the enjoyment and contemplation of culture. Public spectacle and display lie at the heart of the Baroque, and are part and parcel of its innate sense of theatricality. It is striking how many different facets of seventeenth-century life are linked by

an emphasis on the performative and the theatrical. Preacher, actor and poet declaim their words in church, theatre and academy; the king and his court with their carefully staged-managed etiquette are mirrored in the performances and sets of the theatres in the Buen Retiro and the Alcázar; the elaborately staged Church processions with their ornate floats carrying life-like statues of Christ, and the public trials of heretics (the *autos de fe*), avidly watched by king and commoner alike, amount effectively to the Church putting on a performance of its power and authority in matters spiritual. (The painting by Francisco Rizi in the Prado depicting an *auto de fe* in 1680 brings home how the *auto* was very much a public spectacle, showing as it does the enormous banks of spectators and the balconies of the Plaza Mayor in Madrid full of courtiers and officials as well as the King, Queen, and Queen Mother.) Contemporaries quite consciously use theatrical metaphors to describe both Church and state: a 1624 account of an *auto de fe* refers to the 'tablado y teatro de su desdicha . . . en la Plaza Mayor' ('stage and theatre of his misfortune in the Plaza Mayor'), for example, while court eulogists refer *ad nauseam* to the court as a theatre etc.

Such an emphasis on theatricality often reflects an awareness that life is temporary, a mere fleeting performance on the stage of the world, an idea explored brilliantly by Calderón in his allegorical *auto sacramental El gran teatro del mundo* (mid 1630s) in which God becomes the theatrical impresario and the World the prompter, with characters given their roles and props and told to act their parts well, for once they leave the stage (life) their performance will be judged. The metaphor is also made to encompass the whole of (Christian) history, with the World delineating at the start of the *auto* the stages of human history as if they corresponded to the three acts of a typical *comedia*. Furthermore various stages in the account offered by the World (the founding of the first cities, the Biblical flood, and the final cataclysmic destruction of the world at the end of time) are described in terms that consciously evoke the spectacular effects of rapid scene changes typical of the elaborate staging of court drama. In this way, one art form evokes the practices of another, linking court drama and *auto*, Court and creation, king and people in the metaphor of life as theatre.

The omnipresence of the notion of performance, whether literal or figurative, stems in large part from the double perspective which informed the way in which many Spaniards conceived their existences: the temporal perspective and the eternal perspective which also led, as I have mentioned, to the pressing need for *desengaño* and to a belief in the transient nature of life. The transience and insubstantiality of earthly things is one of the greatest clichés of the age. It led to statements like Sor María de Agreda's that 'la filosofía es meditación de la muerte' ('philosophy is mediation on death'), as well as to one of Luis de Góngora's most imitated lines of poetry which describes how physical beauty and life itself turn rapidly 'en tierra, en humo, en polvo, en sombra, en nada' ('to earth, to smoke, to dust, to shadow, to nothing'). Transience and insubstantiality: such ideas lead to a belief in reality as little better than an illusion. What better way to express this than by theatre, an insubstantial world consisting of nothing but illusion?

Further reading:

Ignacio Arellano, *Historia del teatro español del siglo XVII* (Madrid, 1995) – the best introduction to Baroque theatre

Jonathan Brown, *The Golden Age of Painting in Spain* (New Haven and London, 1991) – suberb survey of Spanish art

—, and John Elliott, *A Palace for a King: The Buen Retiro and the Court of Philip IV* (New Haven and London, 1986) – gives a magnificent analysis of court culture

Peter N. Dunn, *Spanish Picaresque Fiction: A New Literary History* (Ithaca and London, 1993) – excellent account of an important genre

John Elliott, *Spain and Its World 1500-1700* (New Haven and London, 1989) – collection of essays on aspects of political and literary life

Henry Ettinghausen, *Francisco de Quevedo and the Neostoic Movement* (Oxford, 1972)

Margaret Greer, *The Play of Power: Mythological Court Dramas of Calderón de la Barca* (Princeton, 1991)

Henry Kamen, *The Spanish Inquisition: An Historical Revision* (London, 1997) – best single introduction to the Inquisition, censorship etc.

Melveena McKendrick, *Theatre in Spain, 1490-1700* (Cambridge, 1989) – excellent chapters on Court drama and the *auto sacramental*

José Maravall, *La cultura del barroco: Análisis de una estructura histórica* (Barcelona, 1975) – a fundamental work but confusing to read with its accumulation of examples

Alfonso Pérez Sánchez, *Pintura barroca en España: 1600-1750* (Madrid, 1992)

Jeremy Robbins, *Love Poetry of the Literary Academies in the Reigns of Philip IV and Charles II* (London, 1997) – offers a consideration of the academy as a social and literary institution

Magdalena S. Sánchez and Alain Saint-Saëns, (eds.), *Spanish Women in the Golden Age: Images and Realities* (Westport and London, 1996)

Paul Julian Smith, *Writing in the Margin: Spanish Literature of the Golden Age* (Oxford, 1988) – stimulating application of literary theory to a wide-range of texts

R.A Stradling, *Spain's Struggle for Europe, 1598-1668* (London and Rio Grande, 1994) – collection of essays offering an assessment of the notion of political decline

Arthur Terry, *Seventeenth-Century Spanish Poetry: The Power of Artifice* (Cambridge, 1993) – wide-ranging discussion of Spanish poetry

Janis Tomlinson, *Painting in Spain: El Greco to Goya* (London, 1997) – basic introduction to Spanish art

II

Appearance and Reality

(1) *Don Quijote*

1. The Impact of Scepticism

Due to its more militant orthodoxy, Spain is often depicted as being entirely backward as regards the development of modern science and philosophy which gradually emerged in the seventeenth century. Such a view is a travesty of the truth, since of all European countries in early modern Europe, it was Spain that confronted most insistently the issues regarding knowledge and perception which lay at the heart of intellectual developments elsewhere in the continent. The difference lies in the fact that Spain confronted these issues primarily via works of fiction. So obsessive are the questions of appearance and reality, of deceit and disillusionment, in Spanish Baroque fiction that such fiction can justifiably be viewed as Spain's major and distinctive contribution to the early-modern preoccupation with knowledge. In this chapter and the next I shall consider the two great works of prose fiction which explore these questions with tireless invention, Miguel de Cervantes' *Don Quijote de la Mancha* (Part 1 1605, Part 2 1615), and Baltasar Gracián's *El Criticón* (Part 1 1651, Part 2 1653, Part 3 1657).

Of course, both *Don Quijote* and *El Criticón* are much more than explorations of intellectual issues. To present *Don Quijote* in particular only in this light is seriously to misrepresent the complexity, humour and diversity of an entertaining and provocative work. Despite such reservations, however, I am proposing to read these works as explorations and responses to the broad intellectual crisis prompted by the rediscovery of scepticism. The degree to which both texts play with notions of perspective, interpretation, error and certainty suggest that both authors are consciously engaged with the key intellectual debate which, historically speaking, served to propel Europe into the modern era: the question of the nature, extent and purpose of human knowledge.

Intense interest in scepticism was occasioned by the publication in Latin of two works by the Classical philosopher Sextus Empiricus (second century AD) in the second half of the sixteenth century. Sextus Empiricus offered a detailed account of a particular type of scepticism, known as Pyrrhonism. This differed from the form of scepticism which had been familiar from the works of another Classical writer, Cicero. Cicero presented a version of scepticism known as Academic scepticism, the main tenet of which was that we know nothing. The Pyrrhonists, in contrast, presented a more extreme version, asserting that we cannot even state that we know nothing since, paradoxically, the statement that we know nothing is itself a positive statement of knowledge. Thus the Pyrrhonists refused to give their assent to any statement, abstaining from categoric judgements and interpretations. Saavedra comments approvingly of this philosophical school, saying that 'cuerda modestia me pareció la de estos filósofos, y no sin algún fundamento su desconfianza del saber humano' (*República literaria*, 1655: 'These philosophers seemed to me to be sensibly modest [in their claims] and not without some foundation regarding their distrust of human knowledge'.)

A key notion which the Pyrrhonists exploited to argue their case was relativism, that is that any human perspective is necessarily relative and limited and cannot therefore claim to offer a definitive and certain interpretation of anything. The need for critical distance to obtain a fair interpretation of a situation was a cliché summed up in Gracián's words 'siempre ven más los que miran que los que juegan, porque no sé apasionan' (*Oráculo manual*, 287: 'those who watch always see more than those who play because they are not emotionally involved'), words which echo those used by one of Zayas' characters quoted in the last chapter. The Pyrrhonists took this notion to its logical extreme, however, arguing that as humans we can never step outside ourselves and therefore can never gain a truly objective perspective.

Both the Academic and the Pyrrhonist forms of scepticism are found in the tantalizing and witty prologue to Quevedo's most serious and moralistic satire, *El mundo por de dentro* (c1612), one of the five *Sueños*, which begins as follows:

> Es cosa averiguada (así lo siente Metrodoro Chío y otros muchos) que no se sabe nada y que todos son ignorantes; y aun esto no se sabe de cierto, que a saberse ya se supiera algo; sospéchase. Dícelo así el doctísimo Francisco Sánchez, médico y filósofo, en su libro cuyo título es *Nihil scitur*, 'No se sabe nada'. En el mundo hay algunos que no saben nada y estudian para saber, y éstos tienen buenos deseos y vano ejercicio, porque al cabo sólo les sirve el estudio de conocer cómo toda la verdad la quedan ignorando. Otros hay que no saben nada y no estudian porque piensan que lo saben todo; son de éstos muchos irremediables; a éstos se les ha de envidiar el ocio y la satisfacción, y llorarles el seso. Otros hay que no saben nada, y dicen que no saben nada porque piensan que saben algo de verdad, pues lo es que no saben nada, y a éstos se les había de castigar la hipocresía con creerles la confesión. Otros hay (y en éstos, que son los peores, entro yo), que no saben nada, ni quieren saber nada, ni creen que se sepa nada, y dicen de todos que no saben nada, y todos dicen de ellos lo mismo, y nadie miente.

> (It is a proven thing, as Metrodorus of Chios and many others have said, that nothing is known, and that we are all ignorant, and even this is not known for certain, but only suspected, for if it was known we'd know something. The very learned philosopher and doctor Francisco Sánchez says this in his book entitled *Nihil Scitur*, 'nothing is known'. In the world, there are some who know nothing and so study to know, and these have good but futile intentions, since at the end of it all their study only serves to reveal that they are ignorant of the truth. Others know nothing and don't study since they think they know it all; many hopeless individuals belong to this group; we

can only envy their leisure and self-satisfaction while weeping over their intelligence. Others know nothing and say they know nothing because they actually believe that they do know something, namely that they know nothing: we must punish their hypocrisy while believing their claim. Others – and I include myself in this worst group – know nothing, don't want to know anything, don't believe anything can be known, say of others that they know nothing, and others say the same of them – and no one is lying.)

Here Quevedo runs through the gamut of sceptical responses, starting with the Pyrrhonist view (represented by Metrodorus of Chios, an ancient Greek philosopher). He continues with the Academic stance (supported by a reference to the Portuguese Francisco Sánchez, a relative of the French essayist and fellow sceptic Michel de Montaigne, and author of one of the most sustained attacks on Aristotelianism from a sceptical position), finishing with a diatribe against human pretensions to knowledge which is akin to much traditional Christian teaching concerning the ignorance of mankind.

Whether or not a reader is familiar with the philosophical arguments of the sceptics mentioned, Quevedo's text lays before the reader their central claims. And the appearance of both forms of scepticism in a satirical work intended for a wide audience indicates how far scepticism had infiltrated Spanish thought by the start of the century. As with many dogmatic moralists, scepticism does nothing to shake Quevedo's confidence in his own moral and religious certainties, nor in pressing their claims upon his readers. Scepticism functions simply as an effective way to shatter human confidence and assurance. In fact, no Spaniard used scepticism against the claims of Christianity, though a few like Gracián came close. Rather, scepticism's greatest impact was to destabilize confidence in Spaniards' ability to gain a true and certain perception and interpretation of the world around them.

Of course it was no coincidence that interest in scepticism intensified during a period of religious upheaval and political uncertainty, for the spread of Protestantism meant that there was no longer a fixed world-order established and stabilized by a single institution, the Catholic Church.

The same period saw confidence shattered from other directions too. Many Europeans were attempting to come to terms with discoveries that had shaken their confidence in the validity and certainty of their own point of view. After the discoveries of the New World – whose 'primitive' inhabitants had led some sixteenth-century individuals like the jurist Francisco de Vitoria in Spain and Montaigne in France to question European presumptions of moral superiority – Europeans encountered Japanese and Chinese cultures whose sophistication was such that even European arrogance could not ignore their cultural and intellectual achievements. Similarly, scientific discoveries such as the gradual realization that the earth revolved around the sun unsettled previously firm convictions.

The result was what can justifiably be called a culture of doubt. This doubt took various forms depending on whether it found expression directly or indirectly and in works of moral philosophy, political theory, history or literature. However it tended to centre around certain key issues which included the following: (1) the status of the knowledge we possess – whether it is certain or provisional, reliable or unreliable; (2) the restrictions imposed on us by our bodies and minds, and the effect our nature as humans has on the type and degree of knowledge we can hope to obtain; (3) following closely from this, the factors which cause us to misinterpret the information we receive from our senses (e.g. our irrational desires, the lies and deceptions of other people, our perspective on an event and the relativity of our view point, optical illusions etc.); and (4) the practical question of how we might circumvent these distorting factors which lead to error.

As I have already mentioned, few writers in Spain directly tackle the issues raised by scepticism from an overtly philosophical perspective, but when they do they show themselves to be as capable and as original as other writers in Europe in confronting the morass of doubt and uncertainty into which scepticism seemed to propel the individual. Whether in Latin – Francisco Sánchez's *Quod Nihil Scitur* (1581) or Pedro de Valencia's *Academica* (1596) – or in the vernacular – Saavedra's *Idea de un príncipe político-cristiano* (particularly 32, 46, 51 and 78) or López de Vega's *Heráclito y Demócrito* (a work which combines Academic scepticism and Pyrrhonism) – peninsular writers did directly engage with scepticism as a pressing philosophical and intellectual issue. The majority of Spanish writers, however, responded to this intellectual crisis with works of imagination which encapsulate the human dilemmas created by the climate of doubt. They did so above all else by obsessively exploring the fraught relationship between reality and appearance. The two works which used the tension between these ideas to maximum effect were *Don Quijote* and *El Criticón*.

2. *El ingenioso hidalgo Don Quijote de la Mancha*

Of all the works produced during the seventeenth century none has had a greater impact than Cervantes' novel about a middle-aged, impoverished gentleman who has his mind turned by reading too many works of chivalry and who decides to set out to recreate himself in the image of a knight-errant and so to recreate the adventures of his fictional heroes. The work is now widely held to be the first modern novel both on account of the profundity of its portrayal of its two protagonists, Don Quijote and his 'squire' Sancho Panza, and because of the extent to which Cervantes reflects upon and ironizes the whole process of writing fiction in the very act of creating a powerful piece of fiction.

There is plenty of evidence to suggest that in the seventeenth century *Don Quijote* was read as a work of humour and parody. This should not blind us either to its serious potential or, more importantly, to the fact that its humour often arises from Cervantes either playing with the serious literary debates concerning fiction or exploiting contemporary intellectual polemics over truth and knowledge. In looking at the novel to see how it exploits issues which, in a different context, were causing contemporaries much intellectual anguish, I shall focus on three interconnected facets: the relationship between *ser* and *parecer*; the erosion of authority and trust; and the tensions between fact and fiction. In different ways each of these areas draws on the debate about knowledge and certainty which so obsessed the early Baroque period.

Don Quijote is described as an 'ingenioso hidalgo' ('ingenious knight') and, like contemporary poets who wrote in the witty style to be considered in Chapter Five, he employs his 'ingenio' ('wit' / 'ingenuity') to forge unusual and striking conceits. One of the most famous examples occurs when Sancho and Don Quijote come across some windmills:

> [D]escubrieron treinta o cuarenta molinos de viento que hay en aquel campo, y así como Don Quijote los vio, dijo a su escudero:
> – La ventura va guiando nuestras cosas mejor de lo que acertáramos a desear; porque ves allí, amigo Sancho Panza, donde se descubren treinta, o pocos más, desaforados gigantes, con quien pienso hacer batalla y quitarles a todos las vidas[.]
> – ¿Qué gigantes? – dijo Sancho Panza.
> – Aquellos que allí ves – respondió su amo – de los brazos largos, que los suelen tener algunos de casi dos leguas. (I.8)

> (They came across thirty or forty windmills that are in that area, and as Don Quijote saw them, he said to his squire: 'Fortune has guided our affairs better than we could have hoped for, since you can see over there, Sancho, some thirty or more terrible giants whom I intend to fight and kill'. 'What giants?', said Sancho Panza. 'Those you can make out over there', replied his master, 'with their long arms – often some of them have arms over two leagues long'.)

The difference of course between witty poets and the 'ingenioso hidalgo' is that as we can see here Don Quijote means his interpretations quite literally. Such misinterpretations draw on a standard argument used in support of scepticism for humorous effect. Sceptics argued that factors like distance can distort the information received by our senses and thus cause us to be deceived – an endlessly repeated example was the square tower which, when viewed from a distance, will appear to be round.

It might be argued that Cervantes is here parodying scepticism by taking one of its key arguments to absurd lengths, yet in the context of the whole novel it seems more accurate to read this as an example of Cervantes literalizing and fictionalizing the terms of the debate about human knowledge and its shortcomings. In embodying some of scepticism's key aspects in such comic adventures an intellectual debate is made more accessible. In contemporary terms the reader is instructed through entertainment, for whether one is aware of the intellectual issues which preoccupied Cervantes' contemporaries or not, it is difficult to read *Don Quijote* and not reflect upon such issues since they form the basis of virtually every episode within the novel.

Don Quijote's misinterpretations of the external world touch upon one of the novel's central themes, the interplay between appearance and reality. Many moralists of the period urged readers to distinguish between the appearance of things and their true essence, between *parecer* and *ser*. Emphasising the hypocrisy of modern life, for example, Quevedo in *El mundo por de dentro* shows us a beautiful woman, only to have the guide, the allegorical figure Desengaño, reveal that her beauty is cosmetic – there is a disjunction between her appearance and what she is really like. The lesson is explained by Desengaño as follows:

> Echo de ver que hasta ahora no sabes para lo que Dios te dio los ojos ni cuál es su oficio. Ellos han de ver y la razón ha de juzgar y elegir: al revés lo haces, o nada haces, que es peor. Si te andas a creerlos, padecerás mil confusiones: tendrás las sierras por azules y lo grande por pequeño, que la longitud y la proximidad engañan la vista.

> (I realize that until now you've never known what God gave you eyes for, nor what their function is. They have to look and your reason

has to judge and make choices: you do the complete reverse, or nothing at all which is worse. If you go around simply believing the evidence of your eyes you'll suffer a million and one mistakes, you'll think the distant hills really are blue and that things in the distance are small, for distance and proximity deceive our sight.)

Reason must interpret the information received by the senses in order to reach a correct interpretation; if not, or if like Don Quijote one is deranged, then an individual will misinterpret reality. Don Quijote's madness makes things appear to him to be different from how they are in reality, and Cervantes uses his hero's madness to take to extremes the human condition portrayed as normal by moralists like Quevedo, namely that we all mistakenly tend to believe unquestioningly our senses, often seeing what we want to see rather than what is actually there. Like such moralists, then, Cervantes is interested in the state or essence of things, and especially in how that essence is ascertained.

The question of when appearances become reality, of when and how our interpretation of the world is both justified and validated, is explored in one of the most famous episodes from the novel which hinges upon the notion of our limited perspective and our reliance on external authority to endorse our perceptions. The episode concerns Don Quijote's helmet. Early in Part I Don Quijote wins in combat a barber's basin which, he proceeds to declare, is a fabulous knight's helmet, the helmet of Mambrino (I.21). Don Quijote christens the helmet after one so named in Boiardo's *Orlando innamorato* (1483, 1495) and Ariosto's *Orlando furioso* (1516, 1532), two of the most influential, light-hearted and widely-read chivalric romances whose early dates indicate just how out-dated Don Quijote's love of chivalric fiction is. When the pair meet up again with the barber, the latter understandably wants his property back. There ensues a discussion as to whether the object is a helmet or a barber's basin. Sancho defends Don Quijote's patently ridiculous interpretation against the barber's patently true one by declaring that it is a *baciyelmo*, a combination of a basin ('bacía') and a helmet ('yelmo') (I.44), and the object in question can function (in part at least) as *both*.

Of course, the basin *is* a basin, but Cervantes' choice of object is deliberately ambiguous in order to focus attention on how we interpret reality via language, since to call the object a helmet makes it have one type of function, while to call it a basin quite another. Can we not therefore legitimately label it as both of these things at once? The 'truth' about the *baciyelmo* seems relative, depending from whose perspective it is viewed, Don Quijote's or the barber's. How, then, do we decide between two competing interpretations if both have a degree of truth? The answer normally is that social practice and convention decides what is true and what is not. Consequently the barber whose basin this is turns to all the people gathered in the inn and appeals to their common sense, confidently expecting that they will support the obvious. He is dumbfounded by their response, for Don Quijote's companions have decided to play a trick for their own amusement. The barber friend of Don Quijote tells the aggrieved barber that the basin is a helmet.

He bases his assertion on grounds much discussed in contemporary debates about the establishment of truth, namely by referring to his personal experience – the fact that he is a barber and has been a soldier. This experience supposedly vouchsafes the truth of his statement. His interpretation is in turn supported by the others present who are in the know, including the nobleman Don Fernando. The fact that his social superiors, 'gente honrada', support the claim that the basin is a helmet throws the barber into a quandary, whether to believe his senses or his social superiors. This comic depiction of contemporary concerns over truth and knowledge then culminates in Don Fernando holding a vote of those present to establish by consensus what the object is (I.45), thereby literally illustrating the social formation of truth. The barber and others not in the know concerning the trick are outraged – understandably, since their social and intellectual superiors are all swearing blind that a basin is a helmet – and a fight breaks out.

What Cervantes raises in the discussion over the helmet is the spectre of a world in which everyone declares that black is white. We are prompted to speculate who in such a world is right, and who is mad, the one person who perceives 'correctly' that black is black, or the vast majority who assert that it is white? Who decides what truth is? Don Quijote himself passes the buck somewhat by bringing up the question of his possible own enchantment by a mean-spirited magician which may affect his judgements. Don Fernando picks up the challenge when he replies that it falls to those present to settle the definition of this matter. But he misses the wider point raised by Don Quijote – how do we know that we are not *all* under a spell and therefore prevented from perceiving the truth?

This issue, perhaps surprisingly, much preoccupied Baroque culture. In Spain it finds its greatest expression in Calderón's metaphor of life as a dream explored in his most famous play *La vida es sueño*. In this play the hero, Segismundo, voices the uncertainty Don Quijote touches upon, for he begins to doubt the reality of his experiences. Finding himself once again in the isolated tower in which he has spent his entire life, he imagines that his experience in the royal palace – where he was taken drugged, unbeknown to him, in order to test whether he was fit to be the ruler of Poland – was simply a dream:

> Yo sueño que estoy aquí
> de estas prisiones cargado,
> y soñé que en otro estado
> más lisonjero me vi.
> ¿Qué es la vida? Un frenesí.
> ¿Qué es la vida? Una ilusión,
> una sombra, una ficción,
> y el mayor bien es pequeño;
> que toda la vida es sueño,
> y los sueños sueños son. (Act 2)

(I am dreaming that I am here chained in prison, and I dreamt that I saw myself in a more flattering state too. What is life? A frenzy.

What is life? An illusion, a shadow, a fiction, and even the greatest
good is small. The whole span of life is a dream, and dreams themselves are nothing more than dreams.)

(In his 1670 *auto sacramental, Sueños hay que verdad son,* Calderón
reverses the notion implicit here that life, being like a dream, is
insubstantial and lacking in truth and reality, by treating
prophetic dreams which, by their very nature, depict truth and
reality.) Descartes draws on the same cultural preoccupation
when he begins the *Méditations* with the hypothesis that the world
was created by a malign spirit who falsifies our every perception;
in such a scenario Descartes is forced systematically to doubt
everything until he hits upon one truth which is beyond doubt,
namely that the act of thinking proves that, at least while
thinking, he exists (the famous *cogito, ergo sum*). Both Calderón
and Descartes are exploring the validity and truth of our experiences.

Of course, Cervantes himself does not go as far as declaring that
there is no truth or that all truth is relative: we as readers know that
the basin is *not* a helmet, that windmills are *not* giants, and that
Don Quijote is *not* sane. The point rather is that such episodes
make us question our confidence in the solidity of our beliefs, as
well as the grounds for our belief in the veracity of the information
which our senses convey to us. In this way we are confronted with
how potentially unstable human knowledge is, based as it is in
large part on the evidence of our senses and on our unfounded
expectations that we can correctly interpret such evidence –
unfounded because we have all at some time or another been
misled by our senses.

What the humour of this famous episode essentially revolves
around is the question of authority and trust. Don Fernando's
social position as a nobleman gives him authority and hence lends
social credence to his assertions – this is what confuses the barber
who cannot understand why the nobleman is declaring a basin to
be a helmet. Reliance on authority of another kind is parodied in

Don Quijote's total trust in and dependence on chivalric fiction. His rigid adherence to chivalric fiction as the one and only authority via which to interpret the whole world parallels one of the prime targets of contemporary sceptics' attacks, namely those dogmatic philosophers who slavishly followed Aristotle, making his texts the basis for their version of reality in all its aspects: both Aristotelians and Don Quijote place written authority over personal experience. Francisco Sánchez, mentioned above, was just one contemporary who used scepticism to attack the prevailing Aristotelian philosophy in this way.

Trust is something which is rigorously dismantled over the course of the novel. It forms the subject, for example, of the inset story, *El curioso impertinente,* which is read out to the group from a manuscript left at the inn (I.33-35). The story concerns two close friends, Anselmo and Lotario. Anselmo marries, and to test his wife Camila's fidelity and honour persuades Lotario to woo his wife, which he does all too successfully, thereby destroying his friend's marriage. Marriage is here presented as a social compact, a bond of trust, and by seeking to go beyond that trust and obtain certainty concerning Camila's fidelity Anselmo breaks the trust that actually constitutes the marriage bond. This cliché is put well by a character in Zayas' *Desengaños amorosos* who acknowledges that 'la fineza del amor es la confianza' (story 2: 'trust is the most noble part of love').

The authority which Cervantes undermines right from the opening chapter is the authority of the text when he systematically sets out to undermine our trust in the veracity of what we are reading. Presenting a supposedly true account, he nevertheless refuses to specify the town in which Don Quijote lives and, more alarmingly, is uncertain as to Don Quijote's real name, declaring, after debating various possibilities (Quijada, Quesada or Quejana), that 'esto importa poco a nuestro cuento; basta que en la narración de él no se salga un punto de la verdad' (I.1: 'this matters little to our story; it's enough that in telling it we never depart a fraction from the truth'). At this early stage the reader is already being made to ponder the nature of truth. Does it require total, objective and accurate information? Can there be truth in the absence of even the most basic and simple of facts? Such uncertainties are nothing compared with the narratorial complexities, all of which are designed to undermine our trust in the text. The story is initially presented by a first-person narrator but this narrator's account stops abruptly at the end of the eighth chapter in the middle of a fight. In the following chapter a further, second, authorial presence appears and tells us of his attempts to find the rest of the story. This he manages to do by accident one day when, in Toledo, he buys a manuscript written in Arabic and gets a *morisco* to translate it into Castilian. (*Moriscos* were Arabs who had converted to Christianity, often under duress, their allegiance to Christianity therefore being treated as highly suspect.) The manuscript itself is by one Cide Hamete Benengeli, an Arab historian, and the story at this point is able to continue, but only by means of the mediation of two individuals whom Cervantes' readers would have seen as innately untrustworthy, the Arab Cide Hamete and the anonymous *morisco* translator. The second narrator who finds the manuscript emphasizes this distrust when he says that Moors are liars and the enemies of all Christians (I.9). Both Cide Hamete, the *morisco*, and the second narrator intrude into the narrative at various points over the course of *Don Quijote* by offering comments on the action or on the manner of its presentation.

What this chain of Arab author, *morisco* translator and several narrators serves to do is problematize the supposed historicity and veracity of the story itself, referred to at various points as an 'historia verdadera' ('true account'), raising thereby the issue of our necessary dependence on, and the reliability of, external authorities as a means of accessing and gauging the truth. Knowledge is seen to be the result of a process of real or potential distortion, and is therefore necessarily always compromised.

If the situation is complicated for the reader, by the second volume of the work it becomes even more so for Don Quijote and Sancho Panza themselves, for Cervantes introduces two twists into the plot. First, the protagonists meet various people who have read the first volume of their adventures. The university graduate Sansón Carrasco, for example, discusses the merits of *Don Quijote* Part I and, more significantly, Sancho and Don Quijote cross-examine Carrasco about their adventures as recounted in order to verify them (II.3-4). To join in the fun, many of these readers go along with Don Quijote's delusions in a more far-reaching way than was the case in the first volume.

For example, Don Quijote meets a Duke and Duchess who have enjoyed his earlier adventures in print and who have decided to use their position and wealth to create a real chivalric illusion in order to amuse themselves with the knight. They transform their palace, their servants and themselves into the world of chivalry. Their obsession with recreating the chivalric world of Don Quijote's imagination causes Cide Hamete to question in turn *their* sanity (II.70). Don Quijote no longer has to impose his vision or version of reality onto the external world since, for the first time, the external world impinges on him a version of reality in which he really is treated like a knight-errant and which really does appear to be like the world of the chivalric romances. This places him and Sancho in a world of deceit and illusion, a world in which appearance and reality are even more at odds than they are in Don Quijote's deranged mind. Again the question of authority and trust as the basis for belief and knowledge is raised acutely by this elaborate deception. To take just one example, Sancho knows that he has never seen Dulcinea (Don Quijote's 'lady') and that he lied to Don Quijote when he stated that he had delivered the knight's letter to her. Knowing this to be true on the basis of his own experience, he is nevertheless thrown into considerable doubt when the Duchess, his social superior and consequently someone supposedly trustworthy, tells him that Dulcinea is as Don Quijote says she is, and that Sancho's misunderstandings come from the fact that he has actually been enchanted (II.33).

Like the *baciyelmo* episode, the chapters dealing with the Duke and Duchess raise the social basis of belief. What does the individual do when others flatly contradict the evidence of their own senses and thereby call into question facts based on personal experience? The dilemma is worse for Don Quijote in so far as he is now presented with a world which mirrors chivalric fiction, prompting the reader to feel increasing compassion for his dilemma. Don Quijote is placed in an identical position to that envisaged by any number of contemporary moralists who declared that humans find themselves in a world of deceit and illusion. The difference for us is that such moralists at least provide a different perspective from which to view the world, and thereby enable us to gain a critical distance on reality from which to question whether what we are confronted with is true or false, *ser* or *parecer*. How is Don Quijote to know that the world around him is mere illusion when there is an all but total match between what he sees and what he expects to see, between outer and inner reality?

What is most interesting is that it is from this point onwards that Don Quijote himself begins to have increasing doubts about his whole chivalric enterprise and identity. No longer in control of his interaction with the world, manipulated by the various situations engineered by the Duke and Duchess, Don Quijote begins more often to question the reality of the chivalric world around him. This is because in a very real sense he is a solipsist, happy to assert his own view of things, but unconfident about supporting the truth claims and interpretations of others. This was an aspect of his character present in the first volume, as when we find him unwilling to support Sancho's claim regarding the packsaddle / horse's trappings while confidently asserting his own ridiculous claim that the barber's basin is a helmet (I.44-45). This solipsism culminates in an episode involving the Duke and Duchess who have constructed a flying horse, Clavileño, which Sancho and Don Quijote mount for a magical journey. The horse, of course, does not move, but Sancho declares that it has flown so high that he was singed by his proximity to the heavens. Adamant in this claim, Don Quijote secretly whispers that he will support this point of view if Sancho in turn will support his own wild claims about having been on a magical descent into the enchanted world of the Cave of Montesinos.

The second twist Cervantes introduces to complicate the protagonists' lives came about as a result of a historical fact. Before Cervantes had published his own second volume in 1615, a spurious volume of the continuing adventures of Don Quijote and Sancho was published in 1614, written by Alonso Fernández de Avellaneda. Understandably, Cervantes was furious at someone else cashing in on the success of his novel. To take revenge, Cervantes has this work too intrude into his own second volume. Don Quijote is first aware of Avellaneda's work when he hears it discussed and learns to his fury that in it he is said no longer to love Dulcinea (II.59). In order to thwart the malicious author who has the knight go to Zaragoza (as was Don Quijote's avowed intention throughout most of Cervantes' work too), Don Quijote decides to go to Barcelona, thereby proving that the account is false. Moreover, he encounters a character from Avellaneda's work, Don Alvaro Tarfe, and makes him sign an affidavit that Avellaneda's heros, whom Tarfe has met, are actually imposters (II.72).

Cervantes thus uses Avellaneda's work to further the humour of his own and to lend a spurious sense of reality to his own characters. Some critics have seen a further twist in this convoluted interaction of two novels, of using fiction to lend a veneer of fact to one's own fiction, in so far as they have argued that Avellaneda was a pseudonym for an Aragonese soldier whose own unpublished autobiography, *Vida y trabajos de Gerónimo de Pasamonte*, finished by 1603, was itself parodied and exploited by Cervantes in *Don Quijote* Part 1 in which the heroes meet a galley slave, Ginés de Pasamonte, who has written an account of his picaresque life to date (I.22). According to this argument, Pasamonte, incensed at Cervantes turning his life into fiction and worsening his character in the process (the real Pasamonte was captured by the Turks and forced to row as a galley slave, whereas the fictional Ginés de Pasamonte is a common criminal condemned as such to be a galley slave), takes revenge by attempting to steal Cervantes' creation. He is then trumped in turn by Cervantes' greater imaginative powers which turned the theft into a further clever twist in Don Quijote's and Sancho Panza's complex relationship with reality.

What these juxtapositions of texts and people explore are the ways in which fiction impinges upon and often substantially actually shapes reality by providing the mental framework by means of which reality is experienced, understood and interpreted. The pernicious effect of frivolous literature, especially on women, was much discussed by over-anxious moralists; St Teresa for one recounts how she was 'led astray' in her youth by voraciously reading too many works of chivalry (*Libro de la vida* [1588], chapter 2). As might be expected given the intrusion of real novels within the text and the incorporation of a variety of genres (chivalric romance, pastoral, picaresque), the nature of fiction is much discussed in the novel. At several points characters debate the merits of fiction, as when the priest and the barber, worried about the pernicious effect of works of chivalry on Don Quijote, conduct a type of literary *auto de fe* on his library (I.6); or when the priest and a canon talk at length about what makes good fiction and why chivalric fiction is bad (I.47-48).

From these debates a number of points emerge. (1) Literary enjoyment is intimately connected with the formal properties of a work. For example, the canon, drawing on contemporary notions of beauty, declares that 'el deleite que en el alma se concibe ha de ser de la hermosura y concordancia que ve o contempla en las cosas que la vista o la imaginación le ponen delante' (I.47: 'enjoyment which is felt in the soul must arise from the beauty and harmony which it sees or contemplates in the things which are placed before it by the eyes or the imagination'). For this reason, chivalric romances are unpleasing, because their plots are incoherent and disjointed.

(2) As with Gracián's theory of wit (Chapter Five), novels should provoke a reaction of wonder and surprise (or *admiratio* as it was

known). As the canon states, they should be written in such a way
that 'facilitando los imposibles, allanando las grandezas, suspendi-
endo los ánimos, admiren, suspendan, alborocen y entretengan,
de modo que anden a un mismo paso la admiración y la alegría
juntas' (I.47: 'by facilitating the impossible, making great things
comprchcnsiblc, and keeping the mind in suspense, they may
cause admiration, suspense, surprise and entertainment, in such a
way that wonder and enjoyment may go hand in hand'). The reaction of listeners within *Don Quijote* to the various stories of other
characters' lives exhibits precisely this range of responses.

(3) The novel should have variety but also an underlying unity
(I.47). The fact that Cervantes himself seems to offer a plot with
too many strands not well integrated into the main story in Part
One is discussed in Part Two of the novel, with Cide Hamete being
accused of unnecessarily introducing the long *novela*, *El curioso
impertinente*, into the first part to avoid the boredom of having
always to write of the two heroes (II.44). Moreover, the *morisco*
translator at one point misses out Cide Hamete's descriptive details
since they are a digression from the plot (II.18).

(4) The final major point concerns a key literary principle that we
will encounter too in *El Criticón*: verisimilitude, the requirement to
give events and characters the semblance of reality. Referring to
the writers of chivalric fiction the canon argues, 'si a esto se me
respondiese que los que tales libros componen los escriben como
cosas de mentira, y que así, no están obligados a mirar en deli-
cadezas ni verdades, responderles hía yo que tanto la mentira es
mejor cuanto más parece verdadera, y tanto más agrada cuanto
tiene más de lo dudoso y posible' (I.47: 'If to all this you reply that
those who write such books [of chivalry] claim that they are lies
and entirely fictional, and that they therefore needn't bother with
finer points or truths, I would reply that a lie is best the closest it
approximates to the truth, and that it causes more pleasure the
more it combines things that are doubtful yet possible').

Verisimilitude as a concept is itself thus intimately connected to the question of *ser* and *parecer* examined so relentlessly on the level of the plot. Don Quijote's problem is that as a reader of chivalric romances he has been so convinced by their fiction that their semblance of reality has become for him reality itself.

Conclusion

The capacity of Cervantes' text to question its own methods, procedures and principles is a further example of its modernity. Yet such techniques are present in many Baroque works which employ the work-within-a-work notion (as in Calderón's *El gran teatro*, discussed in Chapter One) for similar ends, namely to question the relation between art and life, fact and fiction. The difference lies in the fact that Cervantes does this in such an ingenious and knowing way over an entire novel, making so many diverse strands embody this relationship in such an entertaining manner. Taking the types of concerns mentioned at the start of this chapter which were all too real for his contemporaries, he humanizes them in the figure of Don Quijote. He does so not to offer answers to the questions about reality and knowledge which so obsessed the period, but rather to inculcate a sense of tolerance upon readers by unsettling their confidence in the absolute truth and certainty of their own opinions, attitudes and beliefs.

That we laugh at Don Quijote in no way forestalls sympathy for his plight. The plight, while it exaggerates the human condition, is nonetheless recognizably one that preachers, moralists, philosophers and novelists stated was the common lot of humanity: to be stranded in a world of deception in which uncertainty is rife, truth elusive, and trust often entirely misplaced. However in sharp contrast to other contemporaries, Cervantes sets against this pessimistic vision the humanity, comradeship and sheer sense of adventure of Don Quijote and Sancho Panza. In this way, while the impact of scepticism is felt, it is never allowed to overwhelm.

The only other work which shares this supreme capacity to provoke questions and unsettle assumptions is Velázquez's painting *The Family of Philip IV*, otherwise known as *Las meninas* (c1656). As with *Don Quijote*, it is impossible adequately to convey in words the effect of this spell-binding work. The painting presents the viewer with, in the words of Janis Tomlinson, a 'perspectival tour-de-force and a narrative conundrum'. What is the subject? The Infanta Margarita in the foreground, bathed in light and framed by two noble women (the *meninas* of the title); Velázquez himself, poised with brush in hand before a large canvas to the left; or the king and queen, Philip and Mariana, reflected in the mirror at the back of the canvas? (The mirror and the idea of reflection were routinely exploited in art and literature produced for Philip's court, whether in political literature such as Saavedra's *Idea*, or in those court dramas by Calderón in which the court sitting in the palace finds itself reflected in the palace-set on the stage.)

Playing with the notion of perspective, the viewer is challenged by Velázquez in a variety of ways. The mirror's reflection of the royal couple means that the couple 'in reality' occupy a space 'outside' the canvas in the space occupied by us as viewers; their presence is thus evoked in their absence, and the back plane of the canvas is, 'in reality', the plane in front of the actual picture. Compelling the viewer to make the absent king and queen present by hypothesizing their presence outside the canvas, Velázquez emphasizes the power of representation to make present and real what is absent and a mere reflection. If the framed mirror projects our thoughts out beyond the canvas itself into our own viewing space, then the doorway to the right of the mirror projects us in the opposite direction, as we see a courtier climb a stairway. The relation between these two spatial aspects of the canvas, mirror and doorway, is emphasized by the fact that the rectangle of light in the doorway is the same size as the mirror, and that the curtain which is reflected in the mirror is echoed and inverted, as if in a mirror, by the curtain which the courtier on the stairway has drawn back.

This visual conceit which plays with perspective explores the nature of representation and the power of images to work on us almost unconsciously in a way which is analogous to the power fiction has over Don Quijote, the Duke and Duchess, and all the other dozens of characters who react to the stories told over the course of the novel. Both Velázquez and Cervantes use art to challenge, but neither offers ready, easy answers. Their work is compelling precisely because of this. For possible solutions to the issues exploited and explored in *Don Quijote* we need to turn to the other great work of prose of the century, Baltasar Gracián's *El Criticón*.

Further reading:

Daniel Eisenberg, *A Study of Don Quixote* (Newark, 1987)

Ruth el Saffar, (ed.), *Critical Essays on Cervantes* (Boston, 1986) – selection of important essays on Cervantes

Maureen Ihrie, *Skepticism in Cervantes* (London, 1982)

E.C. Riley, *Cervantes's Theory of the Novel* (Oxford, 1962) – indispensable for any serious study of the novel

P.E. Russell, *Cervantes* (Oxford, 1985) – brief but detailed introduction to Cervantes

Leo Spitzer, 'Linguistic Perspectivism in the *Don Quixote*', in *Linguistics and Literary History: Essays in Stylistics* (Princeton, New Jersey, 1948)

Edwin Williamson, *The Half-Way House of Fiction: Don Quixote and Arthurian Romance* (Oxford, 1984) – considers the uses made by Cervantes of chivalric literature

III

Appearance and Reality

(2) *El Criticón*

In *El Criticón* (first published in the 1650s) Gracián approaches
many of the same issues which Cervantes exploits to create the
humorous and thought-provoking episodes of the *Quijote* but from a
perspective which is both more moralistic and more attentive to an
examination of their causes and effects. Gracián seeks to rationalize
and explain why the world is as it is rather than take this as given and
use it as Cervantes does to create endless entertaining confronta-
tions between appearance and reality. In part this is because Gracián
is writing an allegory which as a genre is supposed to be didactic,
and in part it is due to the fact that Gracián is concerned not just to
state the problems inherent in the human quest for truth and certainty but to address how those problems might be alleviated.

That Gracián seeks to alleviate what Cervantes simply presents
as a problem is, as we shall see, an indication of how the intellectual debate concerning knowledge set in motion by the impact of
scepticism had developed by mid-century. *El Criticón* is Gracián's
masterpiece and a tour-de-force of wit. It brings together his views
on human nature and the complexity of the interaction of the
individual with his or her environment as presented piecemeal
across his earlier treatises – *El héroe* (1637), *El político Don Fernando
el Católico, El discreto* (1646), and the *Oráculo manual y arte de prudencia*. In so doing it fuses them into an episodic narrative which
traces the fortunes of two individuals, Critilo and Andrenio.

El Criticón traces the life experiences of Critilo and Andrenio. The
two meet when Critilo is shipwrecked on the island of St Helena and

encounters Andrenio, who has been raised by wild animals and has never seen another human before. The close relationship between the two – they are eventually revealed to be father and son – owes not a little to the example of Don Quijote and Sancho Panza, with the key difference here that Critilo is both older and wiser, and endeavours to correct Andrenio's many mistaken assumptions and misguided actions over the course of the work. The work is structured around their attempts to find Felisinda, Critilo's lover and Andrenio's mother, and this pursuit of an elusive figure (representing Happiness) – the pair are told eventually that she will only be found in heaven – recalls the role of Dulcinea in *Don Quijote*. Both women embody an ideal which gives purpose and direction to life. Although adults when they meet, Gracián subtitles each volume according to the stages in their life: volume one treats their childhood and youth (spring and summer); volume two their adulthood (autumn); and volume three their old age (winter). By linking the course of their lives to the seasons, the lives of these characters are in turn made representative of all lives. The subject of the allegory is life. As Gracián declares in the prologue, the work presents the reader with 'el curso de tu vida en un discurso' ('the course of your life in a discourse').

El Criticón is not so much a difficult work, as one that is written in a genre that is now almost completely alien to modern tastes, allegory. The attraction of allegory lies not least in the fact that by its very nature it operates on various levels; allegory is ideally suited to an age obsessed with *ser* and *parecer*, for it functions by disguising, dressing up, the truth. Thus in reading an allegory, the reader, always aided and prompted by the author, is expected to go beneath the surface-meaning to extract the deeper message, just as in life we are supposed to query appearances to ascertain the reality beneath them. For example, the names of the two central characters, Critilo and Andrenio, indicate their fundamental nature: drawing on Greek words, Critilo's name suggests the faculty of rational judgement, while Andrenio's suggests a person who has more spontaneous and unreflective responses based on passions and desires. As the texts puts it, Critilo's name reflects 'lo juicioso' ('good sense'), Andrenio's 'lo humano' ('humanity'). Two individualized characters in this way represent two contrasting human characteristics.

Similarly, most of the places the pair visit, such as the Court of Falimundo, the Kingdom of Vejecia, or the Plaza Mayor del Universo, are described allegorically. For example, the Palace of Virtelia, who represents Virtue, is reached after escaping from the three sources of sin, the World, the Flesh and the Devil, and after ascending the steep mountain on top of which the palace is built; Virtelia herself is attended by her ministers, the four cardinal virtues Justice, Prudence, Fortitude and Temperance (II.9-10). The work lays great emphasis on allegorical architecture, as can be seen in the description of the palace where Fortune lives:

> se descubría un extravagante palacio que por una parte parecía edificio y por la otra ruina, torres de viento sobre arena, soberbia máquina sin fundamentos. Y de todo el que imaginaron edificio, no había sino la escalera; que en esta gran casa de la Fortuna no hay otro que subir y caer. Las gradas parecían de vidrio . . . No había barandillas para tenerse, riesgos sí para rodar. El primer escalón era más dificultoso de subir que una montaña, pero una vez puestos en él, las demás gradas eran facilísimas. Al contrario sucedía en las de la otra banda para bajar[.] (II.6)

> (They saw before them an elaborate palace which from one angle looked like a building, while from another a ruin, towers of wind built on sand, a proud structure without foundations. And what they took to be a building consisted of nothing more than a staircase, for in Fortune's house one can only go up or down. The steps were like glass [. . .] and there were no banisters, though there was the risk of falling. The first step was more difficult to take than climbing a mountain, but once this was taken, the rest were easy. Those going down, on the other hand, were all too easy to take.)

Outer form here *is* made to reflect the inner essence or truth of the place. Robert Pring-Mill has labelled this style emblematic, since like emblems such descriptions seek to represent 'an intellectual proposition in visual terms'. These set-pieces which occur throughout the work recall contemporary 'arts of memory' which suggested that the reader construct memory palaces in their heads in which they would place symbolic images in the various rooms, the idea being that by wandering around the rooms mentally, the images would be found and the idea they represented would be remembered. Fanciful as it may seem, people did use this as a method to expand their memories. Here, then, by picturing a particular palace the reader immediately also grasps the very nature of the vice or virtue it represents, in this case Fortune.

Gracián's views on allegory as a form of 'sugaring the pill', disguising truth beneath the veneer of fiction or falsehood, are presented in his *Agudeza y arte de ingenio* (1648: chapter 55). Within *El Criticón* itself the question of representation is broached from a number of angles, and the representational concerns we have encountered in Cervantes are present too in *El Criticón*, albeit in a different way. Gracián, for example, wittily addresses the question of our limited perspective and links this to the question of the representation of reality in art by citing an anecdote concerning a painter who came up with a way of depicting a face from all angles:

> Pintó, pues, el aspecto con la debida valentía, y fingió a las espaldas una clara fuente en cuyos cristalinos reflejos se veía la otra parte contraria con toda su graciosa gentileza; puso al un lado un grande y lucido espejo en cuyos fondos se lograba el perfil de la mano derecha, y al otro un brillante coselete donde se representaba el de la izquierda. (III, Dedication)

> (So he painted her from the front with all his skill, and placed behind her in the composition a clear fountain in whose waters was reflected the back of her head with all its grace; and on one side of her he placed a magnificent large mirror in whose depths he was able to show the right-hand profile, while on the other side he depicted a shield in which he showed her left-hand profile.)

The anecdote is lifted from a treatise on art by a rival of Velázquez's, the court painter Vicente Carducho (*Diálogos de la pintura* [1633]), an indication of the proximity of artistic and literary theoretical concerns throughout the period. The difficulty encapsulated here is how to represent reality in its totality. It is important to note that this totality is not naturally perceptible to us in any one act of perception: when we look at a person we do not see him or her from every angle simultaneously. Our perspective is necessarily limited – unless we are lucky enough to find someone placed near a fountain, mirror and a polished shield.

This is a significant issue for Gracián since if we are to discern the essence of something we need to have an undistorted, complete grasp of it. Equally important to note is how the painter necessarily has recourse to artifice to overcome the limitations of human perception. In this way, as Gracián frequently asserts, art supplements nature and can make up for its inherent shortcomings (see, for example, *El discreto*, 18; *Oráculo manual*, 12; and *El Criticón*, I.8).

The distortions and limitations of fiction give rise to perhaps the most significant and baffling statement concerning representation in *El Criticón*: 'no hay cosa más contraria a la verdad que la verisimilitud' (III.10: 'there is nothing more opposed to the truth than verisimilitude'). I mentioned in the previous chapter how verisimilitude was a key notion in Cervantes' theory of fiction. Cervantes' view was upheld by many theorists during the period, the clearest example of the importance of the term to fiction coming in Alonso López Pinciano's *Filosofía antigua poética* (1596) – a work to which Cervantes' ideas are indebted – which states that 'el poeta no se obliga a escribir verdad, sino verisimilitud, quiero decir posibilidad en la obra' ('the poet is not obliged to write the truth in his work, but the semblance of truth [verisimilitude], by which I mean what is possible').

This definition serves to explain Gracián's reservation about the idea of believable fiction (that is, fiction embodying the notion of verisimilitude), namely that it is not concerned with truth. Thus, he prefers a genre which transparently does not seek to deceive with realistic and therefore believable characters and events.

This touches upon one of the deeper paradoxes Gracián seeks to expose: to seek to represent the world realistically (as theorists demanded) is actually to misrepresent the world, since all the artist will achieve is to reproduce surface appearances which Gracián believes have nothing to do with the true reality. Verisimilitude, in this reading, propagates the illusions which it is the moral duty of every person to avoid. A true representation, one that seeks to expose the world as it actually is, will therefore be non-realist in approach. Allegory thus becomes the ideal means of representing truth. As Agudeza advises Truth in the *Agudeza* (55),

> 'que os hagáis política; vestíos al uso del mismo engaño, disfrazaos con sus mismos arreos, que con eso yo os aseguro el remedio, y aun el vencimiento'. Abrió los ojos la Verdad, dio desde entonces en andar con artificio; y usa de las invenciones, introdúcese por rodeos, vence con estratagemas, pinta lejos lo que está muy cerca, habla de lo presente en lo pasado, propone en aquel sujeto lo que quiere condenar en éste, apunta a uno para dar en otro, deslumbra las pasiones, desmiente los afectos, y por ingenioso circunloquio, viene siempre a parar en el punto de su intención.

> ('You must behave like a politician; wear the clothes of deception itself, disguise yourself with its own trappings – if you do this I can guarantee your troubles will be at an end and you will win through'. Truth opened her eyes and from then on deployed various elaborate devices. Sometimes she uses inventions, at others she insinuates herself in round-about ways, conquers by employing various strategies, depicts as far-off what is close at hand, talks of current things by means of past events, brings up in one subject what she wishes to condemn in another, points to one thing to indicate another, dazzles one's passions, contradicts emotions, and by ingenious circumspection always arrives at where she wants to be.)

The telling phrase here is the opening one, 'que os hagáis política' ('You must behave like a politician'). Truth here is being urged to adopt the stratagems of the consummate politician who will employ lies, deceptions and falsehoods for his own ends. Many writers forthrightly disavowed such deception; Joaquín Setanti, for example, states bluntly in one of his aphorisms: 'Ni engañes a nadie, ni te dejes engañar' (*Centellas de varios conceptos*, 117: 'Deceive no one, and do not allow yourself to be deceived'). In sharp contrast to Setanti's disavowal, the closing clauses of the above quotation from the *Agudeza* outline a strategy for Truth which hinges on the deliberate adoption of Deceit.

Truth's strategy recalls the advice offered to the worldly *discreto* in Gracián's treatises like the *Oráculo manual* and *El discreto* who is taught to use circumspection, manipulation and emotional exploitation as the means to success. Gracián thus has Truth adopt the most vilified political idea of the century, the notion attributed to Machiavelli of the end justifying the means. Spaniards like Ribadeneira (*Tratado de la religión y virtudes*) and Quevedo (*Política de Dios, gobierno de Cristo* [1626]) were so virulently anti-Machiavellian that they equated Machiavelli with Satan. And Gracián himself condemns the notion in *El Criticón* (I.10). That Truth must employ deception to make herself known and appreciated is perhaps as ironic a reflection on the fallen state of the world imaginable.

Using illusion to destroy illusion is indeed a curious paradox, but it was one exploited by other artists during the period. Murillo, for example, in his self-portrait (1670 – see the cover illustration) paints a highly realistic portrait of himself within a picture frame (the work-within-a-work idea once again). It comes as something of a surprise to notice that the painter's hand protrudes out of the painted inset frame for no rational reason – the painter is not portraying himself standing behind a picture frame, for example, for the inset frame itself clearly rests on a narrow shelf. The painting challenges by provoking interpretative uncertainty. Similar to the optical illusions so frequently cited by sceptics, the pictorial conceit here is a *trompe-l'oeil*, the painting's stylistic realism momentarily deceiving us into interpreting this as a standard picture of a portrait.

Every episode within *El Criticón* enforces the lesson that the world is never as it seems, and that we need therefore to be vigilant in interpreting every aspect of life so as not to be deceived. This pessimism is reflected in his view of life itself which is presented as a permanent struggle between opposing forces: 'todo este universo se compone de contrarios y se concierta de desconciertos . . . No hay cosa que no tenga su contrario con quien pelee' (I.3: 'the entire universe is made up of opposites and is unified by its divisions . . . Everything has its opposite with which it struggles'). Gracián's view of the world in this respect verges on paranoia: nothing and nobody is as they appear, everyone and everything has something to conceal.

The pessimistic portrayal of the plight of 'natural' man (Andrenio) who is at every turn deceived and led astray is only heightened by the absence of textual references to Christianity. The few references in the opening chapters to the 'Divine Maker' and the like do nothing to lessen the striking fact that in an allegory of life, the Jesuit author has omitted all reference to the truths of Catholicism. The absolute truth of revealed religion was admitted as a kind of certain knowledge by the majority of seventeenth-century sceptics as an exception to our otherwise total incapacity to obtain secure knowledge, but Gracián excludes even this type of truth. The result is only to accentuate the allegory's emphatic scepticism. Man is alone in a world of deception. The nature of a world at conflict with itself is conveyed too in the idea that the world is upside down, 'al revés'. This idea of the reversal of reality, of values being askew which leads to appearances being taken as true, is employed by many moralists such as Quevedo in the *Sueños*. Gracián argues that the topsy-turvy world is a direct result of our failure to employ the one faculty which he believes distinguishes us from animals, our reason:

> es cosa de notar que, siendo el hombre persona de razón, lo primero que ejecuta es hacerla a ella esclava del apetito bestial. De este principio se originan todas las demás monstruosidades, todo va

al revés en consecuencia de aquel desorden capital: la virtud es
perseguida, el vicio aplaudido; la verdad muda, la mentira trilingüe.
(I.6)

(It is striking that although man is a rational being the first thing he
does is to make his reason the slave of his bestial appetites. From this
all other monstrosities of life originate, and as a consequence of such
total disorder everything is stood on its head: virtue is persecuted,
while vice is applauded; truth is silent, while falsehood is trilingual.)

Our human nature is thus blamed for our propensity to misread
reality, and in his depiction of what happens when we refuse to
control our desires and emotions Gracián follows the Stoics in
giving reason pride of place in correcting our misconceptions. It is
this constant endeavour to explain the human condition which distinguishes Gracián's involvement with issues such as perception,
knowledge, *ser* and *parecer* from Cervantes'.

Following his own practice in his earlier treatises like the
Oráculo manual, Gracián fills his allegorical novel with pithy, epigrammatic statements which encapsulate the ideas explored at
greater length within the work's allegorical episodes. Thus, to
convey the notion that human diversity is so limitless that it is
impossible ever to generalize about people, Gracián writes 'Visto
un león, están vistos todos, y vista una oveja, todas; pero visto un
hombre, no está visto sino uno, y aun ése no bien conocido' (I.11)
('If you have seen one lion, you have seen them all, and one sheep
all sheep; but if you see a man, then you have only seen one man,
and have not even understood him very well'). This comment
introduces a chapter entitled 'El golfo cortesano' ('The Courtly
Harbour') in which Critilo and Andrenio enter the Court in
Madrid. The opening words thus prepare us, and the heroes, for
the hypocrisy and deception of all those at court, who appear to be
one thing and in fact are quite another. When Madrid is first seen
in the distance, Andrenio and Critilo typically react in very different ways to what they see, the former optimistically, the latter
pessimistically:

– Veo – dijo [Andrenio] – una real madre de tantas naciones, una
corona de dos mundos, un centro de tantos reinos, un joyel de
entrambas Indias, un nido del mismo Fénix y una esfera del Sol
Católico, coronado de prendas en rayos y de blasones en luces.
– Pues yo veo – dijo Critilo – una Babilonia de confusiones, una
Lutecia de inmundicias, una Roma de mutaciones, un Palermo de
volcanes, una Constantinopla de nieblas, un Londres de pestilencias
y un Argel de cautiverios.

(Andrenio said, 'I can see the regal mother of so many nations, the
crown of two worlds, the epicentre of so many kingdoms, the jewel
of the Indies, the Phoenix's nest and the dwelling place of the
Catholic Sun, crowned with shining gifts and dazzling coats of
arms'.
'Well, I can see', said Critilo, 'a city like Babylon with all its chaos,
Paris with all its filth, Rome with its inconstancy, Palermo with its vol-
canoes, Constantinople with its mists, London with its plagues and
Algiers with its captives'.)

Their reactions thus present two antithetical perspectives on the
essence of what they see before them. Whilst Critilo's interpretations are normally correct, here the truth lies in a combination of
both their views, as their guide El Sabio points out:

– Yo veo – dijo el Sabio – a Madrid madre de todo lo bueno, mirada
por una parte, y madrastra por la otra; que así como a la corte
acuden todas las perfecciones del mundo, mucho más todos los
vicios, pues los que vienen a ella nunca traen lo bueno, sino lo malo,
de sus patrias. (I.11)

'I see', said the Wise Man, 'Madrid, the mother of everything good
when considered from one angle, and a step-mother from another;
for if all that is perfect in the world flocks to the Court, how much
more do all the vices, since those who go there take with them the
worst aspects of their own countries, not the best'.)

The limited perspectives of Critilo and Andrenio, who interpreted
what they saw before their eyes, not according to reason but their

own innate prejudices, are thus corrected by their guide. As so often in *Don Quijote*, so here Gracián bases this scene around the idea of relativity. As I mentioned in Chapter Two, this was another key sceptical notion which was used to argue that it is impossible for humans to gain sufficient objectivity to judge between two differing view points. It is significant that the pair need a guide, someone with a superior vantage point and superior insight, to correct their partial view of the truth; without such guidance, the pair would be locked in their partial and limited perspectives.

In another episode, one guide takes Andrenio onto a hill, to get a different perspective on reality so as truly to understand it since 'lo que no se puede ver cara a cara, se procura por indirecta' (I.8: 'what cannot be seen when face to face can be obtained indirectly'). Driving the lesson home, the same guide adds that to gain the truth about the nature of what we see we must interpret it as the exact opposite of how it appears for 'las cosas del mundo todas se han de mirar al revés para verlas al derecho' ('things in this world must be looked at in reverse in order to see them correctly'). This art of indirection recalls Gracián's allegory in the *Agudeza*, cited above, concerning the means by which Truth must learn to insinuate herself into our minds.

In Gracián's world mankind is confronted with a fleeting world of insubstantial illusions lacking depth and permanence. When Critilo seeks to see Sofisbella, the personification of Wisdom, for example, he is told by his guide that 'todo pasa en imagen, y aun en imaginación, en esta vida' (II.6: 'in this life, everything occurs in images and in the imagination'). This ever-changing, insubstantial world of appearances confronts the individual with major problems, for the very instability of the external world means that true and certain knowledge is impossible to attain. If truth depends on grasping the essence of an object, then in a world of flux truth will always be elusive since our view point will constantly be changing, making objectivity impossible. Consequently, as one guide states, 'de una hora para otra están las cosas de diferente data' (III.5: 'from one hour to the next things appear totally different').

Gracián also identifies the erratic and vacillating character of human nature as a problematic factor in perceiving reality correctly; in the words of one guide, 'ni hay antojos de colores que así alteren los objetos como los afectos' (II.2: 'no coloured spectacles alter how things appear to us as much as our own emotions do'). In other words, our human nature means that our interpretations will always be distorted by our desires and emotions. What we see is more often than not what we want to see. In a sense this is where Don Quijote goes wrong, since he interprets the world according to his innermost desires, namely that the reality be like the world depicted in chivalric romances. The pursuit of truth seems futile. As yet another guide states, 'No hay poder averiguar cosa de cierto' (III.5: 'there is no means of verifying anything with total certainty'). Certainty is thus as elusive an ideal as the pair's quest for Felisinda. Much that is most desired within *El Criticón* – Felisinda, certainty, wisdom – is presented as being like the King and Queen in the mirror in Velázquez's *Las meninas* discussed in the last chapter, an absent presence, a trace, a reflection, since 'todo pasa en imagen' ('everything occurs in images').

Gracián does however present over the course of the allegory a method for beginning to surmount our limited perspective and our human condition: the use of reason. What the guides teach is the necessity for careful, sustained intellectual scrutiny of all the information transmitted by our senses, probing this for inconsistencies, testing it against confirmed experience, and reserving judgement if there is felt to be insufficient information to make an assertion as to what something is. This is the function of the majority of guides encountered who normally correct Andrenio's mistakes, and very occasionally Critilo's, over the nature of the people they encounter and the situations in which they find themselves.

The guides frequently represent qualities of discernment which the characters – and the readers – are supposed to seek to acquire: in the final book, for example, Desengaño teaches the pair to query *circunstancias*, surface phenomena, while the next guide they meet, El Veedor de todo (or El Zahorí as he is also called) goes further by teaching them the skill of looking beneath the exterior to the interior, from *accidentes* to *sustancia*. This suggests a possible way out of the sceptical impasse, for it was a central claim of scepticism that we can only perceive the surface aspect of things (their *accidentes*) not their essence (*sustancia*).

Critilo's procedure is normally exemplary here, for he considers carefully rather than rushing in like Andrenio who bases his opinions and judgements on immediate first impressions only. Even Critilo can err, however, when he allows his innate pessimism to cloud his rational mind, as we saw above in his precipitous opinion as to the nature of Madrid which fails to grasp the full truth about the city. What these slips of Critilo's serve to emphasize all the more is just how arduous a task correctly interpreting reality is; error ensues from the slightest relaxation of one's reason. For Gracián, then, the problem is not so much our lack of knowledge and certainty, as the formidable nature of the highly self-conscious method required to seek a type of knowledge which, if not certain, will at least be as secure as is humanly possible.

The intellectual process Gracián urges upon us is neatly summarized in the following admonition: 'advertid que va grande diferencia del ver al mirar . . . poco importa ver mucho con los ojos, si con el entendimiento nada, ni vale el ver sin el notar' (III.4: 'be warned that there is an importance difference between seeing and looking . . . it matters little if you see a great deal with your eyes if you see nothing with your understanding, nor is looking worth the effort if you fail to notice'). Seeing, in other words, should not be believing. As Critilo urges Andrenio (and through him the reader), '¡Abre los ojos primero, los interiores digo, y porque adviertas donde entras, mira!' (I.7: 'First of all use your eyes, your inner sight I mean, and look closely so that you notice where you are going').

A variety of traditions and concepts fuse here. (1) Gracián's method of rational scrutiny is grounded in Neostoic philosophy which placed great emphasis on reason as a necessary control over our irrational impulses. The ability to control one's self in this way is presented as the hallmark of a gentleman, and is one of the two key factors which serve to distinguish a 'persona' ('person') from a mere 'hombre' ('man'). As Gracián describes this self-control in *El discreto*:

> Una gran capacidad no se rinde a la vulgar alternación de los humores, ni aun de los afectos; siempre se mantiene superior a tan material destemplanza. Es efecto grande de la prudencia la reflexión sobre sí, un reconocer su actual disposición[.] (*El discreto*, 14)

> (Someone of great capabilities never allows himself to give in to his humours and emotions; he always keeps himself above the disturbances caused by the body. Self-reflection, the ability to recognize one's emotional state, is one of the great effects of prudence.)

The other factor which makes someone an individual, a person, is their capacity for, and application of, knowledge, specifically and preeminently, self-knowledge (see, for example, *Oráculo manual*, 4; *El discreto*, 1; and *El Criticón*, I.9). It is worth noting that Gracián consistently views women as incapable of this move towards individuality.

(2) The idea that we need to open our 'inner eyes' quite deliberately evokes Aristotle's definition of prudence, the ability to scrutinize circumstances to select the best course of action, as the 'eye of the soul', and contemporaries often referred to prudence in these terms, as when Andrés Mendo talks of prudence as the 'vista despejada del entendimiento' and as a 'vigilante centinela' (*Príncipe perfecto y ministros ajustados, documentos políticos y morales* [1642]: 'lucid eye of the understanding', 'ever-watchful sentry').

(3) Gracián reworks Jesuit meditational techniques which, as we shall see in the next chapter, placed enormous emphasis on 'la vista de la imaginación' ('seeing with your imagination') – the

careful visualization of every aspect of the subject being meditated upon. Here, this procedure is redirected to a consideration of every aspect of a subject before pronouncing upon it. Every detail, every contingency, is vital if a correct assessment is to be made. This aspect of rational scrutiny is one familiar from Gracián's earlier *Oráculo manual.*

Conclusion

Like much Baroque art, *Don Quijote* and *El Criticón* (if in different ways) are products obsessed with the related questions of truth and representation. All too often however the *Quijote* has been read as primarily engaged with literary precursors – the pastoral, the picaresque, and above all the chivalric romances – rather than as a work which uses these precursors to explore and exploit some of the pressing aesthetic and intellectual issues raised by the loss of confidence in human perception and knowledge which can in large part be traced directly to the impact of scepticism and the split in the Christian Church. Similarly *El Criticón* needs to be read against the background of this debate. The degree to which perception and truth are presented as even more problematic than in the *Quijote* can then also be seen to be a result not simply of style (Cervantes' humour versus Gracián's moral didacticism) but of how the intellectual debate itself had developed by the 1640s and 1650s.

By the mid-century Spaniards viewed *engaño* as endemic in a more acute way than their counterparts in England and France. This was largely due to the manner in which social and political events heightened the intellectual crisis itself, for the 1640s were a bleak decade for Spain: in 1640 Portugal and Catalonia rebelled; in 1643 the Spanish infantry suffered one of their worst defeats at the hands of the French at Rocroi, and the Count-Duke of Olivares fell from power; in 1644 the Queen, Isabel of Bourbon, died; in 1646 the heir to the throne, Baltasar Carlos, died; while in 1648 Spain was compelled to sign a treaty with the Dutch Republic recognizing its full independence and sovereignty. Thus, writers at the very end of the sixteenth century and the start of the seventeenth like the Jesuit Ribadeneira or the picaresque novelist Mateo Alemán, tend to treat deceit primarily in terms of one person tricking another. Gracián, however, views it as enfolding every aspect of life: not only our interactions with one another, but our perceptions, our language, our very beings are inextricably enmeshed in deceit. (It is worth emphasizing that despite his view that 'toda cosa engaña' ['everything deceives'], cited in Chapter One, Alemán only really portrays deceit in his novel as the conscious deception of one person by another, unlike Gracián who really does portray a world in which deceit is an unavoidable part of every level of human existence. In some senses, Gracián shows in detail the alarming consequences of what is only a pessimistic generalization in Alemán.)

Such a conviction as to the omnipresence of deceit makes the quest to limit its damage and try and obtain truth and certainty all the more pressing. Although Descartes proposed that there was indeed one fact beyond all doubt, namely the proposition that 'I think, therefore I am', the majority of Europeans felt, like Gracián, that absolute certainty was simply not possible for humans. The only exception was in matters of revealed religion, and the very absence of this in *El Criticón* only serves to emphasize, as we have seen, the total inaccessibility of certainty for humans.

Given the absence of certainty, it was necessary to develop modes of enquiry to enable people to obtain the most accurate perceptions and interpretations possible. Various methods and procedures were proposed. In England and France the experimental method in science was gradually cultivated and theorized as a reliable source of probable knowledge obtained by dint of repeatable experiments. In Spain, *El Criticón* is typical of the pragmatic approach of many thinkers like Saavedra and López de Vega who sought to inculcate a new mentality as the best means of overcoming, or at least sidestepping, the doubts, uncertainties, and insecurities rife in the wake of scepticism. Gracián's piecemeal explanation and presentation-in-action of this mentality constitutes its fullest portrayal in Spain. To foster a sceptical frame of mind which would query and ponder everything before making any assertion whatsoever about it may not lead to certainty, but it will lead to as secure and reliable a type of knowledge as we are capable of as humans.

It is only at the very end of the century that writers really ceased to view scepticism and its pessimistic teachings about the limits of human knowledge as a critical issue. This shift in attitude can be seen in the century's greatest intellectual poem, Sor Juana Inés de la Cruz's *Primer sueño* (1692), an encapsulation of the debate concerning the possibility of human knowledge which I have suggested is the single most important defining feature of the period. The *Primer sueño* depicts the ambitions of the intellect as it seeks to understand both the entire universe and its creator. It dramatizes the human thirst for knowledge, suggesting this is something vital and unavoidable. Ultimately, though, it presents the pursuit of absolute knowledge as ending in inevitable failure. The major difference from her predecessors comes in the way Sor Juana represents this failure. For Sor Juana the impossibility of gaining essential knowledge of the world is not an obstacle which prevents such attempts from being made, but rather one which simply means that they will fail.

In this way, the impasse created by scepticism – the realization that no certain knowledge of the essence of an object is possible for the human intellect – is simply ignored, and human attempts to discover and to know go on apace. The fact that it is a woman's mind which, while her body sleeps, undertakes the quest for secure knowledge, as is emphatically revealed in the final word of the poem, lends the piece one of its most distinctive and affirmative features. This is all the more marked when the poem is compared with writers like Quevedo and Gracián whose violent misogyny can be linked to their distrust of the body (the feminine being synonymous with the body, just as the masculine was with the mind), a distrust which is itself rooted in their perception of the body as a principal source of deception and, consequently, as the prime cause of our intellectual frailty.

Sor Juana thus reframes the issues concerning knowledge in a way which is quite distinct from the Spanish writers I have treated so far. Unlike them, she sees no need either to create methods which will circumvent or even address the accepted tenets of scepticism, or to justify a continued pursuit of knowledge given those tenets. This is not because she is unaffected or unaware of these, indeed quite the opposite. Rather it is because she has moved on from viewing scepticism as a problem, and has accepted both the ineffectuality of the human desire for knowledge and the inevitability of the quest for such knowledge.

In other words, Sor Juana glories in human attempts to obtain knowledge, rather than wallows in human limitations and hence in failure. It is for this reason that Sor Juana's more level-headed approach can be seen as a distant parallel to European contemporaries such as the English scientists of the Royal Society. Like them she places the search for knowledge as more important – and of more interest – than the philosophical status of any results. As I mentioned in Chapter One, it is precisely for this reason that in the early eighteenth century Sor Juana was cited in Spain as a model for a new form of intellectual enquiry. It is the change in mentality which this shift in attitudes towards knowledge and intellectual enquiry represents which marks the end of the Baroque period.

Further reading:

Baltasar Gracián. Selección de estudios, investigación actual y documentación, Suplementos Anthropos, 37 (1993) – selection of articles on all aspects of Gracián

Karl Alfred Blüher, *Séneca en España: Investigaciones sobre la recepción de Séneca en España desde el siglo XIII hasta el siglo XVII,* translated by Juan Conde (Madrid, 1983) – discusses Gracián's debts to Seneca

Aurora Egido, *La rosa del silencio: Estudios sobre Gracián* (Madrid, 1996) – a stimulating collection of pieces on Gracián

Monroe Z. Hafter, *Gracián and Perfection: Spanish Moralists of the Seventeenth Century* (Cambridge, Massachusetts, 1966) – excellent general study of Spanish moralists

Theodore L. Kassier, *The Truth Disguised: Allegorical Structure and Technique in Gracián's* Criticón (London, 1976) – the fundamental work on Gracián's use of allegory

R.D.F. Pring-Mill, 'Some Techniques of Representation in the *Sueños* and the *Criticón'*, *Bulletin of Hispanic Studies*, 45 (1968), 270-84 – fundamental work on these two key Baroque texts

Paul Julian Smith, *Representing The Other: 'Race', Text, and Gender in Spanish and Spanish American Narrative* (Oxford, 1992) – contains a challenging chapter on allegory

IV

An Art of Impact

(1) Arousing the Senses

As I mentioned in Chapter One, the Catholic Church, following the Council of Trent, consciously began to utilize art (painting and sculpture) in an effort to appeal to the faithful and keep them within the Catholic fold. In Spain, the deployment of art for Christian purposes was most extensively theorized – and practised – by Francisco Pacheco. Pacheco was one of the most successful and influential painters in Seville at the start of the seventeenth century, though he is best remembered now as the master of Diego de Velázquez. A member of an influential academy which devoted itself to intellectual pursuits, Pacheco endeavoured to make art a serious intellectual discipline, and his ideas were expressed in his long treatise, the *Arte de la pintura*. Pacheco emphasized the intellectual side of art by carefully consulting theologians and academics over how certain subjects should be depicted to remain within Catholic orthodoxy: the most famous example of this was the discussion over whether Christ should be shown nailed to the cross with three nails or four (i.e. one nail through each hand and foot). He also offers prescriptions as to how a range of religious subjects should correctly be depicted: St Sebastian, for example, should be shown as a forty-year old man, rather than as a naked youth, not only in the interests of accuracy but also presumably of decorum. Needless to say, no painter followed this reasoning, and Sebastian remained an excuse to depict sensually the nude male body.

In the debate over the degree of preparation necessary in con-

ceptualizing a canvas prior to starting painting, Pacheco followed
the more conservative school who advocated *dibujo / diseño* – the
careful working out of compositional organization via extensive
preliminary drawings – rather than the *colorido* school which
allowed the artist greater freedom to change his mind and alter a
composition during the act of painting itself, producing thereby a
canvas with far freer and looser brush-strokes (referred to by the
term *borrones*). The *colorido* style, practised by Velázquez, requires
that the viewer be positioned the correct distance from the canvas
in order for the composition to be fully appreciated. For example,
another theorist, Antonio Palomino, comments that Velázquez's
brushwork is a miracle when perceived from a distance, but incom-
prehensible close up. The looser *colorido* style thus indirectly
depends upon the notion of perspective which so preoccupied
contemporaries. Pacheco's conservatism makes him argue in contrast that anything capable of close and careful scrutiny is a greater
work of art, whereas a writer like the court artist Vicente Carducho
argues, with certain provisos, that an impressionistic work that
demands distance to be appreciated is more worthy of consideration and praise. (This debate may now seem extremely petty, yet
for contemporaries it was a vitally important question since the
conception of painting as a mental activity (the *dibujo* position)
enabled artists to reason that their work was not simply a manual
skill but was rather a worthy activity for a gentleman. Theory and
practice could thus be linked to social prestige.)

Pacheco's conservatism was not simply a matter of taste, or of a
member of the older generation disagreeing with the innovations of
the younger one. His concerns are at one with his theory of
painting, a theory based on the Church's teaching at this period.
Painting has two key aims: (1) 'parecerse a lo imitado' ('to look like
what is imitated'); and (2) 'apartar los hombres de los vicios' ('to
lead men from their vices'), in order to lead them to the 'verdadero
culto de Dios Nuestro Señor' ('true worship of Our Lord'etc').
Pacheco's emphasis on naturalism had obvious justification given
the didactic function he believes art should play: if the viewer does

not recognize clearly who or what is portrayed, then the picture is unlikely to make him or her dwell on its religious significance. This emphasis on artistic realism finds various parallels in the literature of the period, especially in the picaresque genre, with novels like Mateo Alemán's *Guzmán de Alfarache* giving a stark and vividly naturalistic portrayal of the seedier side of Spanish life: hunger, violence, poverty, and cruelty all being graphically described in an avowedly didactic novel that purports, like religious paintings, to lead the reader towards a better life. In Spanish secular art such naturalism finds expression in the magnificent still life paintings created by Juan Sánchez Cotán and Juan van der Hamen. Exactly how art can lead the mind to God is explained more fully by Pacheco:

> No se puede cabalmente declarar el fruto que de las imágenes se recibe: amaestrando el entendimiento, moviendo la voluntad, refrescando la memoria de las cosas divinas; produciendo juntamente en nuestros ánimos los mayores y más eficaces efectos que se pueden sentir de alguna cosa en el mundo; representándose a nuestros ojos y, a la par, imprimiendo en nuestro corazón actos heroicos y magnánimos, ora de paciencia, ora de justicia, ora de castidad, mansedumbre, misericordia y desprecio del mundo. De tal manera que, en un instante, causa en nosotros deseo de la virtud, aborrecimiento del vicio, que son los caminos principales que conducen a la bienaventuranza.

> (The benefits we receive from images cannot fully be described: they instruct our intellect, move our will, remind us of divine things; they produce thereby in our minds the greatest and most productive effects of anything in the world; they depict before our eyes and at the same time imprint within our hearts heroic and charitable acts, whether of patience, justice, chastity, meekness, charity or rejection of the world. They do this in such a way that, in an instant, they provoke within us a desire for virtue and an abhorrence of vice – the two primary paths which lead to blessedness.)

A religious painting operates on the spectator by activating what were called the three powers of the soul (the intellect, the will, and the memory) each connected with a distinct temporal plane: (i) teaching the intellect (the present); (ii) inclining the will to good acts (the future); and (iii) reminding the memory of divine matters (the past). In this way, religious art is supposed to engage the mind and to link past, present and future into a coherent response to the image contemplated. Visual images are particularly suitable for this process, simply because our imagination is supposedly more captivated by things seen.

To convey this notion Pacheco describes the viewer's senses as being 'violated' by strikingly painted images. Such strong language is not infrequent, and attests to the power contemporaries believed the visual image had over us. A further example of the bodily impact of visual images is offered by Antonio Palomino, the last great Baroque theorist, in his *Museo pictórico y escala óptica* (1715 and 1724). Palomino, who writes of the sacred arrows of religious art piercing the five senses, mentions how a pregnant woman was so affected by the graphic depiction of intense pain in the Spaniard José Ribera's painting of Ixion, pain represented on the canvas by the giant clenching his fists in agony, that she gave birth to a child with withered fingers. He also states that Valdés Leal's paintings for the Church of the Hospital de la Santa Caridad (discussed in Chapter One) provoked such intense horror that people instinctively recoiled with fear on seeing them. However unbelievable, such anecdotes reveal that even at the end of the Baroque period when Palomino was writing there was widespread belief in the power of images to strike the senses in so strong a way as to overwhelm them.

A glimpse of how some individuals might have experienced this theory for themselves is offered in St Teresa of Avila's autobiography where she gives an account of the effect upon her of a polychrome statue of Christ:

Entrando un día en el oratorio vi una imagen que habían traído a guardar, que se había buscado para cierta fiesta que se hacía en casa. Era de Cristo muy llagado y tan devota que, en mirándola, toda me turbó de verle tal, porque representaba bien lo que pasó por nosotros. Fue tanto lo que sentí de lo mal que había agradecido aquellas llagas, que el corazón me parece se me partía; y arrojéme cabe él con grandísimo derramamiento de lágrimas, suplicándole me fortaleciese ya de una vez para no ofenderle. (*Libro de la vida*, chapter 9)

(Entering the oratory one day I saw an image which had been sought out for a particular festival celebrated in the house and was placed there for that reason. It represented Christ with many wounds and was so pious that, as I looked at it, I was overcome seeing him thus, for it showed clearly what he went through for us. So great were my feelings at how badly I had repaid him for those wounds that it seems to me that my heart was splitting; and I threw myself down in front of him with floods of tears, begging him to strengthen me so that I would never offend him.)

Such polychrome statues were produced throughout Spain, and involved the skill of a sculptor to create them and that of a painter to make them even more life-like. They were often placed over altars and in chapels, and were carried through the streets during religious festivals. In St Teresa's response to the statue, we can see that for some people at least theory was translated into practice.

It is worth stressing that Baroque spirituality, centred on the affective response of the individual, had its roots in the writings and 'exemplary lives' of certain sixteenth-century Spanish mystics, above all St Teresa of Avila and St John of the Cross. Both exercised enormous influence across Catholic Europe. On the level of the visual arts alone, Bernini's statue of St Teresa being pierced by a fiery arrow of Divine Love held by an angel – an experience known as the Transverberation – is widely held to be the greatest example of Baroque sculpture. No other work expresses better the plasticity, sensuality and theatricality which characterizes a major strand of seventeenth-century art. Even political theorists like Saavedra Fajardo stressed the power of images to shape morally the character of the individual:

No solamente conviene reformar el palacio en las figuras vivas, sino también en las muertas, que son las estatuas y pinturas; porque, si bien el buril y el pincel son lenguas mudas, persuaden tanto como las más facundas. (*Idea*, 2)

(Not only should the human figures within the palace be reformed but also the inanimate ones, that is the statues and paintings, for although the chisel and the brush are silent tongues, they can be as persuasive as the most eloquent.)

The intensity of much Baroque art, its attempts to stimulate and arouse the senses of the viewer while simultaneously directing them to towards the truths of the Catholic faith, is also often attributed to the impact of the Jesuits. In the *Spiritual Exercises*, a manual written by St Ignatius of Loyola as a series of meditations and exercises to be undertaken over a period of four weeks under the guidance of a spiritual director, Ignatius developed a meditational technique of systematically using the understanding, memory and will, the powers of the soul which Pacheco describes as being worked on by a visual image. The subject-matter has to be vividly evoked by the imagination. For example outlining a meditation on hell, Ignatius has each of the senses dwell in turn on its physicality:

Quinto ejercicio es meditación del infierno. Contiene en sí, después de la oración preparatoria y dos preámbulos, cinco puntos y un coloquio

La oración preparatoria sea la sólita.
El primer preámbulo, composición, que es aquí ver con la vista de la imaginación la longura, anchura, y profundidad del infierno.
El segundo, demandar lo que quiero: será aquí pedir interno sentimiento de la pena que padecen los dañados para que, si del amor del Señor eterno me olvidare por mis faltas, a lo menos el temor de las penas me ayude a no venir en pecado.
El primer punto será ver con la vista de la imaginación los grandes fuegos, y las ánimas como cuerpos ígneos.
El segundo, oír con las orejas llantos, alaridos, voces, blasfemias contra Cristo nuestro Señor y contra todos sus santos.

El tercero, oler con el olfato humo, piedra azufre, sentina y cosas
pútridas.

El cuarto, gustar con el gusto cosas amargas, así como lágrimas, tris-
teza y el verme de la conciencia.

El quinto, tocar con el tacto, es a saber, cómo los fuegos tocan y
abrasan las ánimas. . . .

Fifth Exercise a Meditation on Hell. Consisting of, after the preparatory prayer and two preliminaries, five headings and a colloquy

The preparatory prayer will be the usual one. *First preliminary,* the composition, which here consists of seeing with the eyes of the
imagination the length, breadth, and depth of Hell. *Second preliminary,* asking for what I want, which here consists of asking for a deep
sense of the suffering which the damned suffer so that, should my
faults make me forget the love of the everlasting lord, at least fear of
suffering will help me not to sin. *First heading.* To see with the eyes
of the imagination the enormous flames and the souls with their
bodies of fire. *Second heading.* To hear with your sense of sound the
cries, screams, shouts and blasphemies against Christ and against
his saints. *Third heading.* To smell with your sense of smell the
smoke, sulphur, filth and putrid things. *Fourth heading.* To taste with
your inner sense of taste the bitter things, like tears, sadness and the
gnawing of conscience. *Fifth heading.* To touch with inner sense of
touch how the flames flicker over and burn the souls. . . .)

The key words here are 'composición' and 'la vista de la imaginación'. What is required is that the individual conjure up as vivid
a scene as possible in the imagination of whatever is the subject of
the meditation in order to make the subject matter as real and as
intense to the individual as possible.

The impact of such a technique is twofold. First, in line with
the artistic pronouncements of the Council of Trent, it encouraged vivid and realistic depictions of religious subjects so as to
make these impinge as dramatically as possible on the viewer –
martyrdoms, for example, were depicted in graphic detail, with
the viewer being spared nothing of the instruments of torture,

the beaten and tormented human bodies, the blood and the pain of the saint in question. Ribera was at the forefront of this stark and unrelenting portrayal of pain and torture with a degree of realism that can border on the repellent. His various renderings of the martyrdom of St Bartholomew spare the reader little in terms of the agony of the saint as his body is flayed alive by his amused and inanely grinning torturers. Second, Jesuit meditational practices encouraged the spectator or reader towards an intense scrutiny and empathetic consideration of the subject-matter depicted. A sustained contemplation of the graphic reality of the Saint, Biblical event, or Christian subject portrayed was presumed to be a normative part of the reception of religious art. The Jesuit emphasis on intense scrutiny influenced non-religious writing too, as we saw with Gracián's *El Criticón* (Chapter Three).

Seventeenth-century fiction offers many parallels to the power of images over the senses which we have been considering in relation to art. One of the most striking examples occurs in Miguel de Cervantes's short story, *La fuerza de la sangre*, taken from his collection the *Novelas ejemplares* (1613). In the prologue to this collection, Cervantes emphasizes the utility of his fictional stories as well as their decorous nature in a way which parallels Pacheco's Counter Reformation views on art. He explains, for example, that he has called them 'exemplary' since 'si bien lo miras, no hay ninguna de quien no se pueda sacar algún ejemplo provechoso' ('if you look closely there is not one from which some profitable example cannot be drawn'), and stresses that since they are 'honestos y agradables' ('decorous and pleasant'), they will harm neither body nor soul.

These comments need of course to be placed within the context of contemporary theories of literature which emphasized that fiction (poetry and prose) should entertain and instruct (*deleitar* and *enseñar*), and often conveyed this moralistic notion via the image of surface and depth, the juicy fruit containing a kernel of truth. Whether Cervantes' stories instruct, and in what ways they might instruct are questions that have long preoccupied critics. Here, my purpose in looking at *La fuerza* in the context of the Baroque emphasis on the involvement of the senses is rather to consider some of the problems inherent in such contemporary aesthetic and literary theories, and hence to highlight the dangers inherent in placing sensory arousal at the centre of an artistic style.

In *La fuerza de la sangre* we are confronted with an explicitly happy ending which has the female character, Leocadia, happily marrying Rodolfo, the man who some years previously abducted and raped her, leaving her to face social disgrace and bring up the child who is the result of the rape on her own. This problematic ending is brought about by a whole sequence of fortuitous events which bring Leocadia in contact with Rodolfo's family. His family accept their grandson, and Rodolfo's mother stage-manages a scene on her son's return from Italy to compel him to marry Leocadia – Leocadia appears before Rodolfo for the first time since the rape and the impact of her appearance overwhelms him. The scene thereby enacts and literalizes contemporary artistic theory. (A similar episode of visual apotheosis occurs at the ending of another of Cervantes' stories, *La señora Cornelia*.) At this stage Rodolfo neither recognizes Leocadia nor knows who she is:

Venía vestida, por ser invierno, de una saya entera de terciopelo negro llovida de botones de oro y perlas, cintura y collar de diamantes. Sus mismos cabellos, que eran luengos y no demasiado rubios, le servían de adorno y tocas, cuya invención de lazos y rizos y vislumbres de diamantes que con ellos se entretenían, *turbaban la luz de los ojos que los miraban*. Era Leocadia de gentil disposición y brío. *Traía de la mano a su hijo, y delante de ella venían dos doncellas alumbrándola con dos velas de cera en dos candeleros de plata.*

Levantáronse todos a hacerle reverencia, como si fuera alguna cosa del cielo que allí milagrosamente se había aparecido. Ninguno de los que aquí estaban embebecidos mirándola parece que, de atónitos, no acertaron a decirle palabra. . . . Rodolfo . . . decía entre sí: «. . . ¡Válame Dios! ¡Qué es esto que veo! *¿Es por ventura algún ángel humano el que estoy mirando?*» (My emphasis)

(As it was winter she entered wearing a long gown of black velvet covered with gold and pearl buttons and with a belt and collar of diamonds. Her hair, long and not too blonde, served as her head-dress and its loops and curls decorated through with diamonds *dazzled the eyes of everyone who looked at her.* Leocadia looked and behaved in a pleasing way. *She led in her son by the hand, and two maids went in front of her carrying two wax candles in two silver candle-sticks.*

Everyone got up to pay homage to her as if she were something divine which had just miraculously appeared. None of those present could say a word as they simply stood looking at her, dazzled and stunned. . . . Rodolfo said to himself, 'My God! What am I looking at? *Could it be an angel in human form?'*)

Cervantes, like most seventeenth-century writers, does not offer descriptions gratuitously – they are there to make a point. Here, as is clear from the sections highlighted in the quotation, Leocadia is being presented in such a way as to recall vividly and unmistakably images of the Virgin Mary. She is surrounded by burning candles, bedecked with lavish jewels and arrayed in expensive clothing and all these details bring to mind church polychrome statues and images of the Virgin. Cervantes leaves us in no doubt that this is in the minds of those present, for they react to her as if before a sacred image. Symbolically, this association serves to emphasize Leocadia's innocence and purity; like the Virgin, her pregnancy leaves her blameless of carnal passions, for not only is her son conceived as a result of rape, but she actually faints before the rape is committed.

The iconic association between Leocadia and the Virgin is also designed to work an effect on those present. Cervantes, in fact, shows how Leocadia and Rodolfo's mother consciously deploy the power and force of representation to create the effect theorized by

Pacheco and other writers. The impact of Leocadia's Virgin-like presentation and appearance strikes forcibly the senses of those present. They are overwhelmed by what they see. The effect on Rodolfo, an out-and-out sensualist, is particularly marked. His senses are inflamed; the image of Leocadia 'takes possession of his soul'; and, when Leocadia faints, Rodolfo's overwhelmed state of mind is conveyed by the fact that he stumbles twice in rushing to help and then faints himself. Here, then, we see theory put into practice by Cervantes. Rodolfo's mother, knowing his love of beauty and his sensual passions, deliberately inflames his senses and desires so as to bring about a marriage between her son and Leocadia.

The story thus reveals both Leocadia and Rodolfo's mother to be the embodiment of the key virtue of prudence, knowing when to act and when not to, and it goes without saying that Leocadia also personifies the virtue of constancy. In fact, the combination of human ingenuity in arranging a scene designed to play on Rodolfo's human nature, and trust in God to make all good in the end, exemplify one of Gracián's aphorisms which, attributed to Ignatius of Loyola, states that 'Hanse de procurar los medios humanos como si no hubiese divinos, y los divinos como si no hubiese humanos' (*Oráculo manual*, 251: 'Search out human means as if divine ones did not exist, and divine ones as if human ones did not exist').

On one level then Leocadia and Rodolfo's mother simply make the best of a bad situation, exploiting the power of representation to inflame Rodolfo's passion and lead him into a marriage which provides both a personal happy ending for Leocadia (who loves Rodolfo) and a socially happy one for her, her parents and her illegitimate son. In this way *La fuerza* seems, as many critics have argued, to be a celebration of the institution of marriage as the best means of righting human wrongs and correcting human weaknesses. Cervantes' intention has thus been interpreted as being to show how God's providence, through a series of 'chance' events and encounters, eventually resolves the situation happily in a tra-

jectory from Fall to Redemption. This certainly fits in with the
story's presentation of Leocadia as an exemplary individual: realizing that she is powerless to rectify her situation, she patiently
trusts God, and this trust is embodied in the story's key religious
symbol, the crucifix she takes from the room in which she was
raped.

Nonetheless, certain problematic elements intrude into the
happy ending: (1) Leocadia loves her rapist by the end of the story;
(2) Rodolfo fails utterly to repent; (3) Rodolfo demands proof,
once he has married Leocadia and discovered who she actually is,
that Leocadia is indeed the woman he raped, despite claiming that
he does not doubt her identity ('alguna señal por donde viniese en
conocimiento entero de lo que no dudaba': 'some sign which
would convince him entirely of what he didn't for a moment
doubt'); and (4) for all the talk of critics that Rodolfo has been
redeemed and has transcended his earlier behaviour, he is motivated still by sexual desire – he has married Leocadia simply
because of her beauty, and once married we are told of his impa-
tience to sleep with her – 'tan grande era el deseo de verse a solas
con su querida esposa' ('so great was his desire to be alone with his
beloved wife').

What are we to make of all this (even granted that some of the
above points are perhaps more unacceptable to a modern reader)?
Cervantes, by drawing so precisely the parallel between Leocadia
and the Virgin Mary, is using this scene to highlight Rodolfo's hol-
lowness and shallow behaviour. Providing the contemporary reader
with a strong hint that the ending may not be all it appears to be,
he inverts contemporary theory as to the proper effect of religious
art and images. As we have seen with Pacheco, aesthetic theory
posited that a visual representation worked on the senses, but after
the senses have been engaged, the will and the intellect were supposed to lead the viewer to a 'deseo de la virtud' ('desire for virtue')
and an 'aborrecimiento del vicio' ('abhorrence of vice').

In the encounter engineered by Rodolfo's mother, however,
Leocadia's 'divine' appearance simply has the effect of leading

Rodolfo's thoughts to bed. The irony is clear: unlike a representation of the Virgin, Leocadia's impact on Rodolfo fails to turn his mind to contrition. Of course, Leocadia is not a religious icon, but the emphatic parallel between her and the Virgin, within the context of an aesthetic theory, widespread at the start of the seventeenth century, which was premised on the capacity of the visual to lead the mind to God, serves to highlight for a contemporary reader Rodolfo's failings, his base and self-centred nature. Critical talk of Leocadia's 'miraculous' effect on Rodolfo thus ignores the fact that such a miracle is highly ironic, totally secular rather than religious, leading as it does to his inflamed sexual desire and his obliviousness to the need for forgiveness.

Cervantes' story with its presentation of the power of images to arouse without necessarily any concomitant religious feeling in the spectator should remind us of the ambivalence of much Baroque religious imagery. This raises more general questions about the nature of Baroque art and our reactions to its extreme sensuality and intense realism. Just as *La fuerza* leaves the reader with a strong sense of unease, so similarly the style, treatment and content of much Baroque religious art leaves the viewer with a sense of disquiet. I have argued that one of the things that most distinguishes the Baroque is its mobilization of the viewer, and this is at its most problematic with those paintings which cause the viewer extreme discomfort because of their subject matter. Such art deliberately places the viewer in the position of voyeur since our enjoyment and entertainment arise directly from the graphic depictions of often highly erotically charged scenes.

Pacheco's objections to depictions of a youthful St Sebastian are a case in point here as it is often impossible to tell whether such paintings are religious or erotic in intent, or whether, most provocatively of all, they are a combination of the two. It is Baroque art's capacity to combine such extremes that makes it so disturbing.

Nowhere is this more pronounced than in paintings which depict gruesome martyrdoms, like those by Ribera mentioned above, which place the viewer in the even more uncomfortable position of gaining aesthetic pleasure from depictions of bodily pain. If this sounds somewhat perverse, then it is worth stressing that the acts of violence shown constitute the visual focus in works of art to which we are supposed to respond aesthetically – that is to say, we are supposed to take pleasure in the paintings as paintings. Whilst we might wish to argue that our aesthetic enjoyment arises from the artist's technique – in Ribera's case his theatrical composition and the intensity of focus achieved through his use of *chiaroscuro* (the pronounced contrast of light and dark), both of which owe a debt to Caravaggio – it is of course ultimately impossible to divorce such techniques from the subject matter they serve to convey.

Religious art of this type plays with various antitheses (pain and pleasure, body and soul) often expressed via the facial expressions of the saint and his torturers: in some versions of the martyrdom of St Bartholomew by Ribera, for example, the saint's face is calm and directed at heaven, while his torturers frequently leer out of the canvas at us as viewers, mocking in a sense our own contemplation and discomfort in the scene depicted. In a Christian reading of such paintings, pain is not so much negative as positive, since it serves to reveal the saint's heroism and the soul's consequent salvation. Such paintings attempt thereby to alter our human perspective on matters such as suffering, reversing the normal state of affairs which sees suffering as an entirely negative thing, for what these paintings emphasize is that future spiritual pleasure is guaranteed the saints in question in proportion to their present physical pain. Faith thus transforms the martyr's physical pain into spiritual delight. In a similar paradoxical manoeuvre, the artist makes the martyr's pain an integral source of our own aesthetic pleasure.

This paradox – pain as a source of various types of pleasure and enjoyment – is often condemned by modern critics when encountered in the art and literature of the period as it is so alien to what we like to see as our own more compassionate sensibilities. It is worth remembering here how the Baroque saw such aspects of life as sources of pleasure and amusement. Many of the most avowedly amusing scenes of Alemán's *Guzmán de Alfarache* and Quevedo's *Historia de la vida del buscón, llamado Don Pablos* (1626) depict the child protagonists being beaten, starved, tricked and humiliated. Similarly, Don Quijote was taken as primarily a humorous character, whereas we tend to read his mental delusions, beatings and failures as a kind of philosophical comment on the hardships of life itself.

Such pleasure need not preclude compassion, but to ignore this side of Baroque culture is to ignore one of its central paradoxes – the provocation of conflicting emotions and attitudes within the viewer / reader, and the playing off of these against each other. The disconcerting nature of Baroque art results from this refusal to separate pain and pleasure, sensory enjoyment and religious or moral message. The effect is to attract body and soul. The risk is that the attraction to the former may prevent the latter from responding as theorists wanted. Either way, the individual is challenged to respond. As we shall see in the next chapter, the Baroque challenged not only the senses, but also the mind, taxing it with difficulties that compel it to take an active role in the production of meaning. In an age of uncertainty, creating an impact on the individual becomes a prime means of making him or her seize the initiative.

Further Reading:

Jonathan Brown, *Images and ideas in Seventeenth-Century Spanish Painting* (Princeton, 1978)

Ruth El Saffar, *Novel to Romance: A study of Cervantes's Novelas ejemplares* (Baltimore, 1974) – the fundamental work on the *Novelas*

Alban Forcione, *Cervantes and the Humanist Vision: A Study of Four Exemplary Novels* (Princeton, 1982) – contains a superb reading of *La fuerza* emphasizing the religious context of the story

Gridley McKim-Smith, Greta Andersen-Bergdoll and Richard Newman, *Examining Velázquez* (New Haven and London, 1988) – technical analysis of this painter's technique, but includes an excellent and accessible introductory chapter on the *colorido / dibujo* debate in Spain

Emilio Orozco Díaz, *Manierismo y barroco* (Madrid, 1988) – examination of
the impact of religious literature on Spanish art

Francisco Pacheco, *Arte de la pintura*, edited by Bonaventura Bassegoda i
Hugas (Madrid, 1990) – the introduction to this edition provides an
excellent discussion of Pacheco's text

Jeremy Robbins, 'Spiritual Pain: Ribera and the Visual Representation of
Suffering', in *Belief and Unbelief in Hispanic Literature*, edited by Helen
Wing and John Jones (Warminster, 1995) – explores further the
paradox of depicting pain artistically

Stanislav Zimic, *Las Novelas ejemplares de Cervantes* (Madrid, 1996)

V

An Art of Impact

(2) Challenging the Mind

As well as fostering art which aimed to arouse the senses, the Baroque created a style of literature which aimed to challenge the mind. To do so it consciously employed difficult and recherché language, concepts and syntax. The result is a style which engages the reader to the full, forcing him or her into active engagement with the text to wrest meaning from it. This style is examined in Baltasar Gracián's treatise the *Agudeza y arte de ingenio*, first published in 1642 (under the title of the *Arte de ingenio*) and greatly expanded in the definitive 1648 version which included many more examples drawn from Latin, Italian and Spanish. The *Agudeza* is a very difficult work, but it is worth coming to terms with its ideas as these give a real insight into what one of the greatest prose writers of the century understood of the taste, style and objectives of many of the writers of the period.

The treatise aims to analyze wit (*agudeza*), the name given to the style of writing that I am describing. Gracián presents *agudeza* as something innately Spanish. In order to analyze it, he categorizes a whole variety of conceits (*conceptos*), the conceit being the primary vehicle of wit. Gracián's famous definition of the conceit is concise – and not very illuminating: 'es un acto del entendimiento, que exprime la correspondencia que se halla entre los objetos' (*Agudeza*, 2: 'an act of the intellect which expresses a correspondence which exists between objects').

What does Gracián mean by this description? At first, such a definition seems to include any run-of-the-mill metaphor: noticing a similarity between a marble column and a long, smooth neck, I can create a relationship between the two by referring to a person's neck as a column (to cite a clichéd example from contemporary love poetry). Gracián's comments on his examples make it clear that the conceit is normally something more than this, for the conceit is consistently presented as evoking within us a certain type of response: the words Gracián uses time and again to describe this reaction are surprise, wonder, and amazement. These can be caused by the audacity and ingenuity of the writer's imagination and imagery, or equally by the difficulty or the novelty of his style.

The following lines from Luis de Góngora's *Soledades* (c1613) exemplify these aspects in their striking comparison between the islands in the Pacific Ocean and the bodies of bathing nymphs:

> De firmes islas no la inmóvil flota
> en aquel mar del Alba te describo,
> cuyo número, ya que no lascivo,
> por lo bello agradable y por lo vario
> la dulce confusión hacer podía,
> que en los blancos estanques del Eurota
> la virginal desnuda montería,
> haciendo escollos o de mármol Pario
> o de terso marfil sus miembros bellos,
> que pudo bien Acteón perderse en ellos.

(I will not describe to you the motionless fleet of secure islands in that eastern sea, whose sheer numbers, not through lasciviousness but through their agreeable beauty and their variety, could create the same pleasurable confusion as that caused by the naked white hunting nymphs in the white pools of the Eurotas with their limbs like reefs of Parian marble or of polished ivory, so great that Acteon managed to lose himself completely in them.)

From the convoluted syntax of the opening lines (the prosaic order would be 'no te describo la inmóvil flota de firmes islas en aquel mar'), to its use of Classical myth and its suggestive and surprising comparisons, this extract typifies the style of writing

examined by Gracián in the *Agudeza*. The first image is itself novel
and unexpected: in a speech about the maritime discoveries of
Iberian sailors, the Pacific spice islands discovered are themselves
referred to as an immobile fleet of ships. Further, by means of the
unusual comparison which follows in which the islands in the sea
are likened to the limbs of bathing nymphs, the poet ingeniously
links the feelings of the first sailors who came unexpectedly across
the Pacific spice islands with those of the mythical figure Acteon
who came unexpectedly across the goddess Diana bathing naked
with her nymphs: the sight of both the virgin nymphs and the vir-
ginal islands invoke a sense of forbidden and dangerous desire.
Acteon was turned into a stag and attacked by his own hunting
dogs as a punishment, and this unstated punishment fits in turn
with the tone of the speech from which the lines are taken which
warns of the lust for wealth which the discovery of the New World
awakened in Spaniards.

When the *Agudeza* states that the faculty of the mind which creates conceits (the *ingenio*) aims in so doing not simply to express
truth but also to create beauty (*Agudeza*, 2), it claims something
more for such conceits than that they simply be novel, ingenious
and striking. That a literary device might aim to be beautiful is not
surprising (though Gracián means something quite precise here,
as I shall discuss below); that it might express truth seems now a
more unusual claim.

What Gracián appears to be hinting at is that the turn of mind
which creates conceits uncovers a universe of otherwise hidden
links and correspondences between things in the external world.
The *ingenio*, via the conceit, unifies intellectually a world of otherwise disparate and distinct entities.

How far Gracián meant such a claim to be taken is unclear. But
many seventeenth-century writers shared the view expressed by Sor
Juana Inés de la Cruz which Gracián's statement hints at, namely
that 'todas las cosas salen de Dios, que es el centro a un tiempo y
la circunferencia de donde salen y donde paran todas las líneas cri-
adas' (*La respuesta*: 'all things come from God who is both the

centre and the circumference from which all creation comes and to which it all leads'). Such a Neoplatonic view rests upon a belief in occult links between the terrestrial and the celestial world, with all creation joined harmoniously in the mind of God. Such divine harmony between every element of creation led the Italian theorist of wit, Emmanuele Tesauro, to state that both God and Nature produce conceits (*Il Cannocchiale Aristotelico*). Wit on this reading thus becomes a means of holding together a world which was increasingly falling apart as new scientific and philosophic ideas changed Europeans' perception of reality.

Far more important than Gracián's brief mention of truth is his emphasis on the conceit creating and embodying beauty, something which lies at the heart of his conception of why wit is so pleasing to the intellect. When Gracián talks about beauty, he means something more than simply the pleasing impact many Baroque images have on the mind's eye, as when Gabriel Bocángel creates an arresting image of Leander swimming across the Hellespont to meet his lover Hero, comparing the circular motion of his arms as he swims to the circular tail of a peacock, the eyes on the peacock's tail being like the droplets of water through which the sun shines to create an iridescent effect:

> Agil se otorga al agua sosegada,
> y cuanta arroja el brazo, el pie la hereda;
> pavón cerúleo, deja dibujada
> ojosa espuma en cristalina rueda. (*Fábula de Leandro y Hero*)

(Lithe he throws himself into the calm water, and as much water as is thrown up by his arm, his foot forces back into the sea; an azure peacock, he draws with his arms a watery semicircle sparkling with eye-like droplets.)

From Gracián's explanations of why such conceits cause pleasure it is clear that he believes that there is something quite precise in this type of language – other than its capacity to create a superb image in the mind – which is the cause of its beauty. To understand his thinking on this point we need briefly to consider contemporary views on the notion of beauty.

According to Classical and contemporary theory, beauty arises from the proportional harmony found or created between the constituent elements of an object. As Juan Eusebio Nieremberg wrote:

> se ha de advertir que lo que hace más graciosa y amable a la hermosura corporal es, según todos los filósofos, la proporción de partes bien ordenadas, de suerte que la orden, la cual es propia de la razón, es lo que agrada y hace hermoso, y así no hay hermosura sino en las cosas en que pueda haber orden. (*Tratado de la hermosura de Dios* [1641])

> (What makes bodily beauty more graceful and attractive is, as all the philosophers state, the proportion of well-ordered parts, so that order, which belongs to the reason, is what pleases and creates beauty. Thus, there is no beauty if things lack order.)

Although Nieremberg is discussing physical beauty, the precept of proportion embraced all the arts. In effect, proportion was the key point in all artistic and literary theorizing.

Following this idea, for Gracián the relationship between terms linked within the conceit creates a form of intellectual beauty. We might say that the ideas and objects joined in a conceit are like the columns of a Greek temple, and just as we enjoy the proportional relationship between such columns in a temple, so our minds appreciate the relationship between the ideas and objects brought together by the conceit.

This connection between wit and beauty becomes clearer when we consider an analogy established by Gracián: 'lo que es para los ojos la hermosura, y para los oídos la consonancia, eso es para el entendimiento el concepto' (*Agudeza*, 2: 'what beauty is to the eye and harmony to the ear, the conceit is to the mind'). That is to say, what creates beauty for the eye is proportion, for the ear consonance, and for the mind, the conceit. Via such analogies Gracián relates both the formal structure of the conceit and the pleasure its reception causes the mind to the principles of harmony and correspondence.

One of the conceit's functions, then, is to embody beauty on an intellectual or abstract level via the unusual and ingenious correspondences between separate objects. In the lines cited above by Bocángel in which Leander's actions while swimming are described in terms of a peacock's tail, the impact of such a conceit would have been attributed by Gracián to the neat correspondences drawn between arms, water, tail and patterned feathers, the mind taking pleasure in the relationships thus expressed.

To take another example, it was a cliché to describe a woman's curly hair as being like the sea. Such a comparison is based on a correspondence of similarity between hair and waves – both undulate. This proportional correspondence is worthy of being called a conceit once further novel and ingenious elements are added to the original image as happens in the first stanza of a love sonnet by one of the period's great poets, the Count of Villamediana. Imitating the Italian poet Giambattista Marino, who in turn was imitating the Spaniard Lope de Vega (an example of the extent and complexity of imitation across languages in this period), Villamediana extrapolates further resemblances between other objects associated with the original image: if the woman's hair is like waves, then a comb becomes a ship, the hand holding the comb is the hand steering the vessel, and sighs the wind which fills the ship's sails:

> En ondas de los mares no surcados,
> navecilla de plata dividía;
> una cándida mano la regía
> con viento de suspiros y cuidados.

(The little silver boat divides the waves of uncharted seas; a white hand steers it with a breeze of sighs and sorrow.)

The proportional relationship between the terms is almost mathematical: sea is to boat as hair is to comb, the metaphor arising when items from the first relational pair (sea / boat) are interchanged with the second (hair / comb).

It is these ingenious links between items so obviously otherwise unconnected (sea / boat and hair / comb) which Gracián saw as pleasing to the mind. Moreover, it is precisely these figurative links that some saw as conveying otherwise hidden connections between disparate elements within creation, thereby expressing a deeper truth about the harmony of the universe.

In brief, then, a conceit is a novel, ingenious or surprising image which links its constituent terms into a variety of relationships, sometimes based on similarity sometimes on dissimilarity, these relationships endowing the image with what was believed to be a requisite of beauty, namely proportion, thereby causing pleasure to the mind, the intensity of such pleasure being directly related to the novelty, ingenuity and wonder of the image itself.

One of the most remarkable and difficult poems of the Baroque is Góngora's *Fábula de Polifemo y Galatea* which exemplifies the way poets sought to challenge, surprise, and, especially, delight the mind in the ways that Gracián theorizes. Góngora is the Spanish poet most cited by Gracián in the *Agudeza*, and his two great poems, the *Polifemo* and the *Soledades*, created an enormous impact when they were first circulated in manuscript in the early 1610s.

Góngora's style divided his contemporaries. Even in an age which emphasized that great art was synonymous with elite art, his many detractors, who included the two other great Baroque poets Quevedo and Lope de Vega, accused him of creating obscure and unnecessarily complex poetry. The poet and painter Juan de Jáuregui epitomizes the feelings of Góngora's detractors in his description of the errors of poets who followed the new style:

> huyendo esta sencillez y estrecheza, porfían en trasponer las palabras y marañar las frases de tal manera, que aniquilando toda gramática, derogando toda ley del idioma, atormentan con su dureza al más sufrido leyente, y con ambigüedad de oraciones, rev-

olución de cláusulas y longitud de períodos, esconden la inteligencia al ingenio más pronto. (*Discurso poético* [1624])

(Fleeing this simplicity and narrowness, they insist on transposing words and mixing up clauses in such a way that destroying all grammar and overthrowing every linguistic rule, they torture the most long-suffering reader with their harsh style, and hide their meaning even from the most astute mind beneath the ambiguity of their phrases, the chaos of their clauses and the sheer length of their sentences.)

Despite such criticisms, even Góngora's enemies were affected by his stylistic innovations to the extent that the critical cliché that Góngora represents one style (*culteranismo*) and his great enemy Quevedo another (*conceptismo*) is simply not tenable: there are stylistic differences, but both poets strive for the same aesthetic qualities which Gracián stresses – novelty, ingenuity, wonder and surprise – sometimes achieving this primarily by their use of language (*culteranismo*), sometimes by the nature of the concepts (*conceptismo*).

The *Polifemo* is a reworking of a Classical myth which describes how the hideous one-eyed giant Polyphemus, jealous of Acis who has won the heart of the nymph Galatea, crushes his rival to death with a rock, only for Acis to be transformed into a river. From this material* Góngora creates a masterpiece. The sensuous nature of his language and the tortuous quality of his syntax ideally suited this story of idealized beauty and violent passions.

Much of the lyrical intensity of the poem is due to its commingling of harmony and disharmony, both on the level of plot and of language. As far as the subject matter of the poem is concerned, the coexistence of order and chaos is more than evident.

---

* Familiar to contemporaries both from Classical sources such as Ovid's *Metamorphoses* and from versions by other Spanish poets such as Luis Carrillo y Sotomayor (a poet known for the complexity of his poetry, and whose version Góngora is clearly, and successfully, trying to surpass).

Polyphemus' hideous looks and destructive jealousy contrasts sharply with the idealized beauty and the harmonious, idyllic pastoral world of the young lovers. As for the language of the poem, many of its clauses are beautifully ordered and symmetrical. But it is clear that such symmetry and proportion are only possible because Góngora makes great use of the rhetorical figure known as hyperbaton, the breaking of standard word order for the purpose of effect. It is this perfect fit between style and theme that makes the *Polifemo* possibly the greatest poem in Spanish.

In a poem much concerned with beauty, proportion and harmony permeate the *Polifemo*, revealing how Góngora strove to make the poem an embodiment of beauty. On the immediate visual level the work is striking for the number of carefully balanced, symmetrical clauses it employs. The majority of stanzas, for example, contain lines such as the following:

gimiendo tristes y volando graves. (stanza 5)
(sighing sadly and flying ponderously)

muerta de amor, y de temor no viva. (44)
(dead from love, and from fear not alive)

o al cielo humano o al cíclope celeste. (53)
(either the human sky or the heavenly Cyclops)

Such rhetorical structures create in their ordering of material visible proportional correspondence between words, phrases and clauses. In the first quotation above, for example, Góngora repeats the sentence structure (gerund / adjective), while in the second he inverts the structure (adjective / 'de' plus noun) in the second clause. And by means of the final negation he makes two normally antithetical terms ('dead' and 'alive') synonymous, linking opposites in a relationship of equivalence which strikes the mind pleasurably with its poetic dexterity. It is this level of ingenuity and linguistic nuance that Gracián and his contemporaries delighted in. These structures consequently literally embody the formal properties of beauty as these were perceived by contemporaries: order, balance and harmony.

Similarly, on the aural level, even the smallest unit in the poem, the vowel, is made to yield balance and order. The patterning of vowels within lines and across stanzas mirrors the symmetrical disposition of the poem's words and clauses. This aspect of the *Polifemo* has been studied in great detail by C.C. Smith. To cite just two examples, which I have left untranslated as they are meaningless without their context, in the line 'la caverna profunda, que a la peña' (stanza 5) the opening vowels, a-a-e-a, are repeated at the close of the line; while in the line 'Galatea lo diga, salteada' (38) the opening vowels, a-a-e-a, are inverted at the close, a-e-a-a. Whilst a familiar feature of Spanish poetry, this vowel patterning is taken to new and extreme lengths in the *Polifemo*.

The features of the *Polifemo* so far mentioned contribute considerably to the plasticity of the poem and work on the reader almost subliminally. They also contribute to the peculiar sense of tautness with which the poem is imbued, with many of its conceits holding opposites in tension such that the mind takes pleasure in the way that an image fuses contradictory elements, as in the stanza describing Galatea's complexion:

> Purpúreas rosas sobre Galatea
> la Alba entre lilios cándidos deshoja:
> duda el Amor cuál más su color sea,
> o púrpura nevada, o nieve roja.
> De su frente la perla es, eritrea,
> émula vana. El ciego dios se enoja,
> y, condenado su esplendor, la deja
> pender en oro al nácar de su oreja. (14)

(Dawn drops on Galatea petals from deep red roses and brilliant white lilies, such that Love cannot decide what colour her cheeks are, either snowy rose or red snow. The Red Sea pearl competes in vain with the whiteness of her forehead. The blind god Cupid is annoyed and so condemns its splendour, hanging it in gold from her mother-of-pearl ear.)

In a characteristic manoeuvre Góngora presents Galatea's complexion as the fusion of opposites, with the line 'o púrpura nevada, o nieve roja' presenting, via its symmetrical clauses, two alternative interpretations which are, in fact, identical.

Also striking is the closing conceit based on a correspondence between an ear and a shell: Galatea's ear, being shell-like in colour and shape, is the natural place to find a pearl, especially one whose own beauty and colour she surpasses. This imagery emphasizes her beauty as well as the fact that she is a sea-nymph. Describing how such poetry creates its effect inevitable fails. Even so, seeing wit in practice, as here, reveals how ingenuity and rhetorical dexterity can fuse to create supremely beautiful and arresting poetry.

Baroque prose also exhibits the stylistic characteristics discussed by Gracián. A major influence here was the Roman writer Seneca whose distinctive style grew in popularity over the opening decades of the century as his Stoic philosophy became increasingly influential. Seneca's sentences are full of puns, word-play etc., while his clauses and sentences tend to be short, epigrammatic, and lack conjunctions to join them together. The result is a staccato style, in which the individual units are more prominent than the harmonious effect of the whole.

The most venerated Classical authority, Aristotle, had stated that the 'periodic' style was both pleasing and easy to commit to memory, which goes some way to explain why the epigrammatic style of Seneca so appealed to an age concerned with impact and instruction. Seneca's style contrasts sharply with Cicero's style, emulated in the sixteenth century, in which long, flowing, carefully interconnected clauses and sentences create smooth and accessible prose.

Gracián's prose typifies the Senecan style; Cervantes' is more akin to the Ciceronian approach; while a writer like Saavedra (whom I will consider in the next chapter) tends to combine the two styles, mixing short, pithy sentences – which importantly encapsulate his central ideas – with longer, more structured sentences in the Ciceronian mould.

Gracián himself is the prime example of a writer whose prose sought to embody aesthetic qualities intended to challenge the mind. In the *Oráculo manual y arte de prudencia*, a collection of three hundred aphorisms which influenced French writers like La Rochefoucauld and Madame de Sablé and from which I have already quoted, Gracián's style is at its most elliptical and epigrammatic. (He gives his views on aphorisms and the like in the *Agudeza*, 29.) Others before him had written aphorisms, like the Catalan Joaquín Setanti (*Centellas de varios conceptos*) or the major political theorist Baltasar Alamos de Barrientos (*Tácito español*) whose debts to Tacitus indicate a further stylistic source of this particular genre. But nobody had produced a work in which style was as important as substance, something Gracián discusses within the *Oráculo* (see aphorism 14 for example).

Like the epigram, Gracián's aphorisms strive to create an immediate effect and do this by creating arresting and wittily expressed 'truths' or insights into the human condition. Thus, the statement 'Nadie mira al sol resplandeciente, y todos eclipsado' (169: 'No one looks at the sun in all its glory, but everyone does when it's eclipsed') embodies the psychological truism that we all focus on human failure more than success in such a memorable way that the rest of the short aphorism is really a redundant gloss on this one line.

As in the example just cited, sentences and clauses are kept short. And throughout the collection great use is made of wordplay, and especially certain rhetorical features such as 'paronomasia' (the use of words which are similar in sound but different in meaning) and 'polyptoton' (the repetition of a word in a different grammatical form). These two rhetorical features can be seen in the following examples, though by their very nature they are all but impossible to translate:

No cansar. Suele ser pesado el hombre de un negocio, y el de un verbo. La brevedad es lisonjera, y más negociante: gana por lo cortés lo que pierde por lo corto. Lo bueno, si breve, dos veces bueno; y aun lo malo, si poco, no tan malo. ... (*Oráculo manual,* 105)

(Don't be a bore. The man with one concern is a bore, as is the one with only one theme. Brevity flatters and opens more doors: it gains through courtesy what it loses through brevity. What is good, if brief, is twice as good; and even bad things, if short, are not so bad.)

No es necio el que hace la necedad, sino el que, hecha, no la sabe encubrir. Hanse de sellar los afectos, cuanto más los defectos. Todos los hombres yerran, pero con esta diferencia: que los sagaces desmienten las hechas, y los necios mientan las por hacer. Consiste el crédito en el recato más que en el hecho, que si no es uno casto sea cauto. ... (126)

(The fool is not someone who does something foolish, but someone who, once this is done, cannot hide it. Keep your emotions locked up, and even more your defects. Everyone errs, but with this difference: wise men deny what they have done, while fools blab about what they are about to do. Reputation is more a matter of caution than of actual deeds, for if you can't be chaste than at least be cautious.)

In both we see examples of 'paronomasia' ('cortés' / 'corto', 'afectos' / 'defectos', 'desmienten' / 'mientan', 'casto' / 'cauto') and 'polyptoton' ('lo bueno' / 'bueno', 'necio' / 'necedad').

What these two figures so favoured by Gracián create is a sense of minor orthographical changes marking major conceptual shifts in meaning. Many Baroque writers employ similar conceptual play which conveys the sense of the instability and mutability of reality via the way in which one term can be transformed into its real or figurative opposite ('milicia' / 'malicia'; 'dicha' / 'desdicha'; 'ocio' / 'negocio'; 'Eva' / 'Ave'; 'desaire' / 'donaire', etc. ['militia' / 'malice'; 'happiness' / 'unhappiness'; 'leisure' / 'business'; 'Eve' / 'Ave'; 'slight' / 'gracefulness']). The Baroque predilection for word-play of all descriptions is thus one manifestation of the period's fascination with mutability and flux.

Such word-play is graphically described by Gracián as being like the mythological multi-headed monster the hydra, which would spring two or three new heads every time one of its existing heads was removed (*Agudeza*, 31). This encapsulates the fascination with conceits of this kind, for diversity of meaning springs from a single source. The immediate overall effect of such rhetoric is to keep readers on their toes, since mental agility is required to prise the meaning from such laconic sentences. That Gracián values this aesthetically can be seen in the first aphorism above when he flatly declares that 'lo bueno, si breve, dos veces bueno' ('What is good, if brief, is twice as good').

The *Oráculo* is presented as a collection of adages designed to enable the elite to succeed in a world in which *engaño* is rife. The projected reader is the *discreto*, so called because of his superior powers of perception and discrimination, who is required to learn the 'art of prudence', prudence being synonymous with the scrutiny of events, actions, and people to discern their true causes and motives.* This ideal individual is the subject of aphorism 49 in which Gracián eulogizes the '*Hombre juicioso y notante*' ('discriminating and observant man'):

Señoréase él de los objetos, no los objetos de él. . . . En viendo un personaje, le comprehende y lo censura por esencia. De raras observaciones, gran descifrador de la más recatada interioridad. Nota acre, concibe sutil, infiere juicioso: todo lo descubre, advierte, alcanza y comprehende.

(He rules over objects, rather than they over him. . . . Seeing a person, he grasps and judges their very essence. Of singular powers of observation, and a great decipherer of the most hidden depths. He records harshly, thinks subtly, reasons acutely: he discovers, notices, grasps and understands everything.)

*(The *discreto* is always presented by the intensely misogynous Gracián as a male figure, and was the subject of a separate treatise by Gracián, *El discreto*, in which the reader's task of extrapolating the author's meaning and intention is further complicated by the work's juxtaposition of different types of discourse – allegory, satire, dialogue, panegyric, letters, etc.)

What underpins all this is the Baroque obsession with appearance and reality. Where many writers endeavour to teach how to avoid the former so as to obtain the latter, Gracián's attraction lies in the seemingly amoral way in which he rather teaches the *discreto* how to exploit appearances on the basis that 'las cosas no pasan por lo que son, sino por lo que parecen' (99: 'things do not pass for what they are, but for what they appear to be').

This sentiment is reiterated in aphorism 130, but in such a way as to make clear that what Gracián is recommending is that an individual take advantage of this fact of life, either to manipulate the gullibility of others or, what is perhaps more sinister, to pass oneself off as something one is not:

> *Hacer y hacer parecer.* Las cosas no pasan por lo que son, sino por lo que parecen. Valer y saberlo mostrar es valer dos veces: lo que no se ve es como si no fuese. . . . Son muchos más los engañados que los advertidos; prevalece el engaño y júzganse las cosas por fuera. Hay cosas que son muy otras de lo que parecen. La buena exterioridad es la mejor recomendación de la perfección interior.
>
> (Do and also seem. Things do not pass for what they are, but for what they appear to be. To outshine and to know how to show it is to outshine twice; what is not seen might as well not exist at all. . . . Those deceived are far more numerous than those in the know; deceit is everywhere and things are judged only by their exteriors. There are things which are actually very different from what they appear to be. An impressive exterior is the best way of suggesting a perfect interior.)

This may seem fairly innocuous, but what would have struck contemporaries would have been the work's neglect of Christian ethics in pursuit of worldly advantage.

In presenting his art of prudence in human terms as if a divine frame of reference were both unavailable and irrelevant (to paraphrase the terms of aphorism 251), Gracián secularizes the key Christian virtue of prudence to a far greater extent than occurs in Catholic works of statecraft in which the term plays a central role.

In matters political and moral Gracián is a true pragmatist, realizing that the mode of idealized conduct presented as the objective in the many books of conduct and behaviour written during the period presented an ideal unattainable in a corrupt and fallen world. Rather than ignore reality, he teaches how to confront it on its own terms so as to succeed.

The basis of Gracián's strategy for worldly success is aesthetic, resting on the notions of wonder, novelty, and surprise which he analyzes as key components of literary style in the *Agudeza*. (The link with the *Agudeza* is discernible too in the deployment of adjectives such as 'sutil' and 'juicioso', used in aphorism 49 cited above, which recur throughout the *Agudeza* to describe both conceits and writers.) These concepts occur repeatedly over the three hundred aphorisms (of particular importance here are numbers 3, 25, 45, 81, 85, 94, 95, 133, 170, 181, 211, 212, 269, and 282).

They form an essential part of a strategy for the successful domination of the *discreto*'s environment since Gracián reasons that most people follow what they admire, and that what evokes the greatest degree of admiration is anything new. Anyone wishing to exercise control over others needs therefore constantly to evoke wonder. Thus he advises the reader not to reveal all his qualities at once, nor to lay all his cards on the table, so as to be able to keep a degree of suspense and expectation.

The impact of novelty and wonder is conveyed in a telling analogy when Gracián says that 'un alfiler pudo conseguir estimación, pasando de un mundo a otro, y un vidrio puso en desprecio al diamante porque se trasladó' (198: 'a pin became highly prized moving from the Old World to the New, and a glass bead was worth more than a diamond'). This example draws upon Spanish experience in the New World, illustrating the power of novelty to provoke wonder, and offers an example of how this can be exploited to the advantage of the 'superior' intellect. For Gracián therefore the aesthetic principles of wit also form the basis of his worldly ethics. In this way a literary style becomes a way of life.

If the *discreto* is envisaged as a member of a social and intellectual elite, then the reader too is required to possess the same
intellectual agility as the *discreto*. The linguistic difficulties with
which the reader of Gracián's prose, or indeed Góngora's poetry,
is confronted are a deliberate obstacle to immediate and easy com-
prehension. Such difficulty was much debated by contemporaries.
Those advocating stylistic complexity tended to argue that it
heightened the readers' pleasure by making them become actively
involved with the text, as well as making the text itself inaccessible
to all but the intellectual elite.

Linguistic difficulties aside, aphorisms by their nature are a frag-
mented form of knowledge, requiring readers not only to unravel
the meaning of each individual maxim, but then to construct sense
and coherency from the whole. In an age which, as a result of the
impact of scepticism, saw the gradual erosion of confidence in the
human capacity to obtain true and certain knowledge of the world,
the aphorism was a literary form ideally suited to express the ten-
tative, partial and fragmentary nature of human knowledge which
was believed to be all that was obtainable.

The popularity of aphorisms throughout the century is thus in
large part due to the problematization of knowledge occasioned by
scepticism. Aphorisms require us to read creatively and to engage
actively in the production of meaning since an interpretation is
not presented to us on a plate. It is as if we are given the bricks and
mortar, but lack the architectural plans necessary to turn these into
a house.

The form of the *Oráculo* thus challenges the reader to create
unity from diversity, coherency from many apparent contradic-
tions, for uncertainty regarding the writer's intention demands
deeper reflection. What, for example, is the reader supposed to
make of an aphorism like 247 whose second sentence indirectly yet
flatly questions the assumption presented as absolute in the first:
'*Saber un poco más y vivir un poco menos. Otros discurren al contrario*' ('*Know a little more and live a little less. Others argue the
opposite*')? Such moments make interpretation a kind of game.

Indeed, as in so much seventeenth-century writing, Gracián conceives of the self and its strategic actions as a game (196, 238, 240, 287).

In a supposedly didactic genre, this ludic emphasis and its lack of categoric assertion throw readers back onto their own mental resources: we have to make up our own minds. Consequently, the *Oráculo* is a typical product of a sceptical age in so far as it raises more questions than it seeks to answer, and its difficult style together with its elusive form mean that our minds are challenged just as much as our wits are stretched.

As I have argued throughout this chapter and the previous one, part of what is distinctive about the Baroque is the way that it sought to captivate the senses and the mind of the individual. Baroque art and literature demands a response. A response which is personal and so engaged. There is no half-measure with such art and literature, no means of keeping our distance, for the Baroque developed a style in the face of which a passive reaction is simply not possible.

This goes a long way in explaining why the Baroque as a style has always provoked such strong reactions, whether positive or negative, both in the seventeenth century as well as in the twentieth, for the Baroque is, above all else, an art of impact.

Further Reading:

Jorge Checa, '*Oráculo manual*: Gracián y el ejercicio de la lectura', *Hispanic Review*, 59 (1991), 263-80 – challenging analysis of Gracián's engagement of the reader's mind

Aurora Egido, *Fronteras de la poesía en el barroco* (Barcelona, 1990) – suberb collection of studies on various aspects of Baroque poetry

Helmut Hatzfeld, *Estudios sobre el barroco* (Madrid, 1964) – contains one of the best analyses of the *Oráculo*'s style

T.E. May, 'An Interpretation of Gracián's *Agudeza y arte de ingenio*', *Hispanic Review*, 16 (1948), 275-300

Nicholas Spadaccini and Jenaro Talens, (eds,), *Rhetoric and Politics: Baltasar Gracián and the New World Order* (Minneapolis and London,

1997) – superb collection of essays, particularly strong on the construction of subjectivity within Gracián's work

Michael Woods, *Gracián Meets Góngora: The Theory and Practice of Wit* (Warminster, 1995) – exacting but thought-provoking analysis of Gracián's theory in relation to the poetry of Góngora

VI

Forming and Performing Identity
Theatre and Court

Much Baroque literature is preoccupied with the formation of a public persona or image. This preoccupation may take the form of role-play within the theatre, or the projection of a poetic presence in lyric poetry, or guidance to the courtier on how to act and behave. The idea of appearance and reality again plays a pivotal role here, for the creation of a persona splits the self into its public and private aspects, and while contemporaries would have argued that the two should ideally fuse – virtuous words and deeds should be matched by true inner virtue – they were realistic enough to recognize that this does not, and cannot, always happen. This gulf between public and private – between, for example, a husband who appears honourable but who believes that he has been dishonoured, or a king who espouses religion but who secretly acts contrary to its teachings – obsessed Spaniards. It is in theatrical and political texts that these problems of enacting and projecting an identity are most relentlessly explored. In this chapter I shall consider a range of issues centred around the notions both of identity as intimately connected with the projection of an image, and of the self as performative, seeing how role-play can be a means of challenging the status quo, and how, given the close identification of king and state, the endeavours of writers of statecraft to educate the ruler and so form his public identity extend to an exploration of Spain's own image and performance. On both the real and the political stage, fashioning an identity and maintaining it successfully depended ultimately on factor's beyond the individual's control. As we shall see, our limited autonomy was perhaps the greatest challenge and the most difficult truth confronting both fictional and real individuals alike.

As I have already mentioned, the notion of performance infused the entire period. Even the most 'natural' and 'sincere' type of literature, love poetry, is in reality the result of a conscious performative act which aimed to convince by deploying a rhetoric of sincerity. Love poetry was almost always written in the first-person singular. Following the example of Petrarch, Spanish love poets like Quevedo, Góngora, and Lope de Vega made the projection of this textual image of the suffering poet-lover the primary focus of attention.

Such poetry aimed to offer the reader an intimate glance at the purported emotions and passions of the poet. Rhetorical manuals taught how to deploy language to maximum effect. The appearance of spontaneity and sincerity was in this way the result of a careful and calculated use of rhetoric. The poet, like a successful actor, had to project a persona and make his emotions appear credible and sincere and in so doing make the reader forget that, in the vast majority of cases, both persona and emotions are the product of artifice rather than personal feeling. That the sincerity and credibility which were the hallmarks of Petrarchan love poetry were the result of a successful 'performance' is made transparent in literary academies where poets wrote verse on amatory topics which were set by the secretary, the resulting Petrarchan persona clearly having nothing to do with personal involvement, or real life experiences.

I mention love poetry because it is a form of extended self-creation and projection in which the success of the poem is tied in many ways to the credibility of the performance, and these ideas of self-creation, projection, and credibility are central to both the theatre and the court. The notion of credibility of performance was urged upon real people (by Gracián in the *Oráculo manual* for example), and credibility was also, as we shall see, very much an issue of state in manuals of statecraft. Similarly, the self-conscious-

ness and self-awareness of love poets in their manipulation of amatory personae were very much echoed in the theatre, where
characters frequently adopt other roles and identities within plots.
It is this dimension of the theatre – the way it frequently comments
upon and exposes contemporary culture's fascination with and
dependence upon performance and self-projection – which makes
it such a fruitful starting point for a consideration of identity in the
Baroque.

1. Theatre

Baroque theatre presents no clear division between the individual
and society, between the body and the body politic. The individual
is always conceived of as a social entity, and playwrights dramatize
the alarming way in which the body is never autonomous but,
rather, a space defined by the multiple and conflicting discourses
of sex, religion, politics, and power. Some playwrights portray
these social determinants as absolute, presenting class, for
example, as something innate rather than accidental, and gender
as rigidly and deterministically governing our emotional and intellectual nature. Others suggest that we have a certain potential to
surmount determining factors, often conceptualising this as free
will, while also of course recognizing that the possibilities for self-
determinism are not limitless. These dramatists treat the self as
more contingent and emphasize the notion of human agency.

However, central to any portrayal of the relationship between
individual and society, and complicating that relationship in disturbing ways, is the concept of honour. The popularity of honour
plays was commented on by Lope de Vega in his *Arte nuevo de hacer
comedias en este tiempo* (1609) where he writes, 'Los casos de la
honra son mejores / porque mueven con fuerza a toda gente'
('Matters of honour make the best plot as they never fail to move
everyone'). The capacity of 'casos de la honra' to move rests not
only on the horror produced by the chilling, cold-blooded murders of normally innocent wives (in Calderón's *El médico de su honra*

[late 1620s], for example, the husband has his wife bled to death because he believes she has compromised his honour), but also on the psychological dilemma of the husbands who must choose between murdering their wives or losing their social standing, between love and honour.

The threat of losing one's identity arises because of the way honour is portrayed as structuring the individual's identity. If we divide identity into its private and public spheres, it is the public aspect which alone matters. The public perception of an individual is paramount, and that perception in the theatre rests almost exclusively on the issue of whether someone is perceived as being honourable or not. Honour is thus vital to a sense of self.

Indeed so closely linked are honour and a sense of identity that the loss of honour is experienced as a total loss of self: as one of Calderón's husbands says, in *El pintor de su deshonra* (mid 1640s), 'no soy mientras vengado / no esté' (Act 3: 'I do not exist until I have taken revenge [and so recuperated my honour]').

Honour is so important because its possession signals that one is a member of – since one has been recognized by – the social elite. It is worth noting here that honour is normally presented as the exclusive preserve of the nobility: this is what makes Lope's *Peribáñez y el Comendador de Ocaña* (mid 1600s) so unusual, for its hero is a peasant with an innate sense of his own honour – though significantly, after being pardoned for killing his socially superior rival, Peribáñez is elevated socially by the king who makes him a captain, thereby confirming the view that honour and social status go hand-in-hand. The individual is consequently dependent upon others for the maintenance of his honour status; in Lope de Vega's famous words:

> Honra es aquella que consiste en otro;
> ningún hombre es honrado por sí mismo,
> que del otro recibe la honra un hombre;
> ser virtuoso hombre y tener méritos,
> no es ser honrado.
>
> (*Los comendadores de Córdoba* [early 1600s], Act 3)

(Honour is that which rests with another; no man himself can call himself honourable, for it rests with another to give him such honour; to be a virtuous and worthy man is not in itself to be honourable.)

The result of honour being in the eye of the beholder is that the slightest thing can destroy it. Gutierre in *El médico* phrases this graphically when he addresses honour thus:

> A peligro estáis, honor,
> no hay hora en vos que no sea
> crítica; en vuestro sepulcro
> vivís: puesto que os alienta
> la mujer, en ella estáis
> pisando siempre la güesa. (Act 2)

(You are in constant danger, Honour, every moment is critical for you. You live in your own tomb: since woman gives you life, in her you are always treading on your grave.)

What Gutierre means here is that honour for a married man rests with his wife's virtue and fidelity and, since women are viewed in the Baroque as unstable, irrational and emotional, honour is consequently always in danger of being destroyed because it is placed in such a fragile vessel.

Not surprisingly, in Calderón's plays this view of honour instils in men a fanatical sense of insecurity and panic and makes them highly suspicious and almost pathologically jealous since so much hinges on the maintenance of their honour – their (social) identity. The situation is made worse by the fact that once honour has been called into question, the husband loses his honour. The slightest suspicion that a wife may have been unfaithful is sufficient to destroy honour.

This notion is conveyed in several of Calderón's plays by the image of a cloud passing over the sun:

> . . . nadie puede
> borrar fama tan segura
> ni opinión tan excelente.

Pero sí puede (¡ay de mí!)
que al sol claro y limpio siempre,
si una nube no le eclipsa,
por lo menos se le atreve;
si no le mancha, le turba,
y al fin, al fin le oscurece.

(*A secreto agravio, secreta venganza* [mid 1630s], Act 2)

(No one can obliterate a reputation and a name which is secure and certain. What am I saying? Of course they can, for when a cloud passes in front of it, even the clear and unsullied sun is, if not eclipsed and tarnished, affected and disturbed, and in the end darkened.)

Although the cloud does not permanently affect the sun, it momentarily blots out its light, and from a human perspective this appearance of impurity is sufficient to destroy the sun's / honour's integrity. Paradoxically in an age which, as we have seen, urged individuals to see the reality beneath appearances, where honour is concerned it is only appearance that really matters socially.

As can be imagined, the formulation of a social concept vital to an individual's identity as something all-but out of an individual's hands to maintain leads to men being paranoid about their honour status and predisposed to wipe out any potential stain on their wives' reputations by murder, whether their wives are 'guilty' of infidelity or not. Husbands enter upon a frenzied pursuit of certainty, wanting to discover whether their honour is intact or not, but are forced to confront two aspects of honour: (1) the impossibility of certainty where honour is concerned, for, given that it rests with others to confer it, no individual can secure and control it. Appearances are always capable of being misread and misinterpreted, as we have seen a whole variety of writers assert over the course of this book. (2) The irrelevance of certainty – as I have said, suspicion, the merest possibility of dishonour, is what matters here, not the reality behind the appearances.

This portrayal of the pursuit of something vital but elusive and nebulous has convincingly been linked with the real-life preoccupation with *limpieza de sangre* (purity of blood), the need to have 'pure' Christian blood, not 'tainted' by Jewish or Moorish ancestors, in order to enter any of the organs of state – a religious order, the Church, the military orders, etc.

The analogy is valid, for purity of blood was both out of the hands of an individual and open to be questioned and investigated on the basis of malicious gossip that one's ancestry was not pure. The fact that such purity statutes were hypocritical in the extreme given that the elite propagating them were the social group most likely to have 'mixed' blood in their ancestry did not prevent them being of central importance to sixteenth– and seventeenth-century social institutions.

The obsession with honour as framed within drama of the period is also clearly linked to what I have called the wider culture of uncertainty, for the husband's intense desire for certain and secure knowledge, only to be confronted with the impossibility of that knowledge and the anxieties caused by the resulting doubt, are part and parcel of the diversity of responses by Spaniards to the crisis in knowledge which I considered in Chapters Two and Three. Indeed, the urgent pursuit of certainty is a recurrent feature of the *comedia* that invariably leads to tragedy, as in Tirso's *El condenado por desconfiado* where Paulo brings about his own damnation while striving to know with certainty whether he is saved or not.

The public / private distinction is also often brought into the question of revenge itself. Most husbands seek to take revenge privately, so as not to publicize the dishonour which they believe has fallen upon them, hence the title of one of Calderón's plays, *A secreto agravio, secreta venganza* – Secret Revenge for a Secret Injury. Husbands thus seek to avoid public exposure, but the irony of Calderón's three famous wife-murder plays (*A secreto agravio, El médico* and *El pintor*) is that private revenge ends up being made public. Consequently, while figures of authority condone the husbands' actions once they are made public – the murders in the first two plays are sanctioned by kings (Sebastian of

Portugal and Pedro of Castile) and that in the third play by the Prince of Ursino – their dishonour is nevertheless made known.

In this way, the plays close on an ambiguous note for they effectively exemplify Saavedra's words on the futility of revenge: 'Más honras se han perdido en la venganza que en la disimulación: ésta induce olvido, y aquélla memoria' (*Idea*, 32: 'More people's honour is lost via revenge than by dissimulation: we forget the latter, but remember the former'). I shall return to the question of honour and its public perception when I consider below how honour and reputation were posited as important, if precarious, elements of both the king's and the country's image.

Like male identity in honour plays, female identity was constructed in literature as intimately connected with social reputation. As we have just seen in wife-murder plays, the woman becomes not simply the symbol of her husband's honour, but its living repository: as Mencía, the wife in *El médico de su honra*, states, contrasting her life before and after marriage, 'Tuve amor, y tengo honor' (Act 1: 'Before I had love, now I have honour') – there is no room in marriage for emotion. Marriage places woman in the impossible situation of being synonymous with her husband's honour. The role of women during the period is often entirely symbolic; they are the embodiment of values of paramount importance to male identity (the wives in honour plays); to male aspirations (Felisinda's function in *El Criticón*); and to male ideals (Dulcinea in *Don Quijote*). Women are thus constrained by the necessity to conform to a largely male-defined notion of what a woman should be (passive, chaste, virtuous, obedient etc.).

The major exception was in the theatre where a significant degree of latitude was permitted in two key ways: (1) the development of character types such as the *mujer varonil*, the woman who, whether out of choice or necessity, refuses to conform to (male) social expectations of her; and (2) the fact that in comedies women were permitted a far greater degree of sexual and moral license than in other types of play. Occasionally, too, a playwright will present a woman assuming control of her own destiny in order to achieve a 'laudable' social goal.

Rosaura, in Calderón's *La vida es sueño*, is just such a character. To seek redress for her lost honour, she dresses as a man, travels from Russia to Poland with a servant, and ends up fighting in support of Segismundo's rebellion against his father. In a powerful and charismatic speech she presents herself, with her sword and dagger, to Segismundo and implores his aid, playing on her dual identity as a woman and as a man (in which guise Segismundo first encountered her):

> Mujer vengo a persuadirte
> al remedio de mi honra,
> y varón vengo a alentarte
> a que cobres tu corona.
> Mujer vengo a enternecerte
> cuando a tus plantas me ponga,
> y varón vengo a servirte
> cuando a tus gentes socorra.
> Mujer vengo a que me valgas
> en mi agravio y mi congoja,
> y varón vengo a valerte
> con mi acero y mi persona.
> Y así piensa que si hoy
> como a mujer me enamoras,
> como varón te daré
> la muerte en defensa honrosa
> de mi honor. (Act 3)

(I come to you as a woman to save my honour, and as a man to encourage you in your quest to gain your throne; as a woman, I place myself at your feet to soften your heart, as a man I will stand by your side when you help your people; as a woman I come to ask for your help in my dishonour and distress, and as a man I will support you with my sword and my life. And if you are thinking of taking advantage of me as a woman, I will, as a man, take your life in defense of my honour.)

The critic Melveena McKendrick has described this speech as 'Rosaura's ecstatic bisexual celebration of identity', yet it must also be said that, just as her breaking the social code by dressing as a man is motivated solely by a desire to reenter it by marrying the man who deceived her, so here she upholds gender roles in the very act of exploiting them to gain her objectives. Thus while Rosaura is one of the most dynamic and enterprising women in Spanish drama who, when pushed to extremes, breaks social norms and crosses gender boundaries, she does so not as an act of rebellion but as a means of eventually enforcing these norms once again by regaining her social identity via marriage. To find a truly transgressive portrayal of identity, one that prompts us to query the very notion of identity by presenting it as fluid, we must turn to a comedy, *El vergonzoso en palacio*.

Tirso de Molina's *El vergonzoso en palacio* exemplifies the freedom conferred on women in the name of comedy and depicts one of the theatre's most arresting *mujeres varoniles*. *El vergonzoso* is a daring and fast-moving comedy whose twists and turns arise in large part from the question of identity and the comic possibilities of role-play. The play concerns two sisters, Madalena and Serafina, and the fulfilment and frustration of their desires to select a partner for themselves. Madalena wishes to marry Mireno, her secretary and apparent social inferior, and Serafina falls in love with her own portrait (painted, unbeknown to her, while she is dressed as a man), and her suitor, Antonio, tricks her into believing he is the man in the portrait. As a means of expressing their desire and thus of overcoming the social restraints on women which curtailed the active pursuit of their own agendas, each sister exploits the idea of performance and role-play.

Tirso's play thus makes superb use of the play-within-a-play idea. Madalena feigns sleep so that, watched by the timid Mireno, she can act out her courtship and encouragement to Mireno as if she is dreaming her actions and his responses. In so doing she assumes Mireno's character as well as her own (Act 3). Serafina goes even further by rehearsing a play, *La portuguesa cruel*, which she intends to perform for her sister's amusement – I shall return to this scene below. In a further twist in *El vergonzoso en palacio*'s history, the play itself becomes a work-within-a-work when Tirso incorporates it into his novel *Los cigarrales de Toledo* (1621).

In *Los cigarrales* Tirso mounts a defense of the play against a number of criticisms levelled at it, including that the play was indecorous (comedies, it was felt, should not have Dukes and Counts amongst their key characters), improbable (the fact that Serafina falls in love with her own portrait), broke Classical rules (Aristotle's stipulation that a play's action should all occur in a twenty-four hour period), and portrayed historical Portuguese figures in fictional and unflattering circumstances (the Duke of Coimbra disguising himself as a shepherd etc.). This last point included the accusation that the Duke of Avero's daughters (Serafina and Madalena in the play) are depicted as 'desenvueltas' ('over-confident') and that their actions are consequently 'contra las leyes de su honestidad' ('against the laws of virtue and integrity').

In a very real sense, from the perspective of the seventeenth century itself, it is difficult to argue with this last point. Both daughters break their father's wishes by selecting their partner, and behave even more indecorously by sleeping with them in his house. As a consequence of their actions Madalena ends up with the man she wants; Serafina, in love with her own image, ends up being compelled to marry someone she does not love, Antonio. The impact of such a risqué plot can only be imagined, but we can begin to appreciate Tirso's daring when we consider *El vergonzoso* in the context of the words of Francisco Bances Candamo, a theorist of drama who urges the need for decorum by citing a play by Calderón:

Don Pedro Calderón deseó mucho recoger la comedia *De un castigo, tres venganzas*, que escribió siendo muy mozo, porque un galán daba una bofetada a su padre, y, con ser caso verdadero en Aragón y averiguar después que era el padre supuesto y no natural, y con hacerle morir, no obstante, en pena de la irreverencia, con todo eso

Don Pedro quería recoger la comedia por el horror que daba el
escandaloso caso. (*Teatro de los teatros* [1689-90])

(Don Pedro Calderón greatly wished to withdraw the play *De un castigo*, which he wrote when he was very young, because in it a young
nobleman hits his father. Although this was based on a real incident
in Aragon, and it later turns out that the man is not his real father,
and the son is killed, Don Pedro nonetheless wanted to withdraw
the play because of the horror which the scandalous incident provoked.)

Serafina is the character whose use of disguise and performance is
the more complex, primarily because she dresses up simply to
please herself, not as a means of obtaining a desired goal like
Rosaura in *La vida es sueño*. Her role-play thus assumes greater
depth as it appears that she uses it to express otherwise inexpress-
ible aspects of herself. The fact that Serafina's play, *La portuguesa
cruel*, will take place during carnival allows her a degree of licence
which she seizes and exploits to the full. In the brief extract she
rehearses in front of her servant Juana she plays all the roles, and
does so while wearing full male costume. Carnival time thus allows
her at least to fulfil her desire to dress and behave like a man given
that she cannot be one:

> Fiestas de Carnestolendas
> todas paran en disfraces.
> Deséome entretener
> de este modo; no te asombre
> que apetezca el traje de hombre,
> ya que no lo puedo ser. (Act 2)

(Carnival celebrations always involve disguises. I want to enjoy
myself in this way too; don't be surprised that I fancied dressing as
a man, for the fact is I cannot be one.)

Serafina's performance here both of character and gender is mul-
tilayered. Tirso plays with the notion of performance. Not only
does Serafina play a number of male roles within *La portuguesa*

cruel, but the nature of performance as something requiring an audience is underscored by the fact that she is watched not only by Juana, but by Antonio and a painter concealed in the bushes, and, in turn, by the real audience. Furthermore, that her male disguise indicates deeper psychological desires is hinted at in a variety of ways. For no apparent reason, she chooses to keep her male clothes on under her dress once the performance is over. Seeing her in male clothes, her servant declares that she is so handsome she could fall in love with her/him. And during her performance, Serafina gets so carried away in her male role that she 'mistakes' Juana for one of her female play's characters and embraces her.

The playing with possibilities here is obviously deliberate, but trying to categorize Serafina as, in anachronistic terms, a transvestite, a lesbian or a transsexual seems of less immediate concern than that she relishes the opportunity to behave as a man, in dress, word, and deed. However categorized, it is clear that her sense of self is markedly at odds with all social and sexual expectations of what was deemed normal for a woman.

The exploration and adoption of other identities, and the possibilities this offers of allowing the expression of personal desires and aspirations otherwise forbidden by gender or class, is the driving force behind the entire play. Mireno, for example, is unhappy with his identity as a shepherd, feeling he is cut out for a more noble role. To give form to these aspirations he first assumes the identity of Ruy Lorenzo, secretary to the Duke, and subsequently of Don Dionís, under which guise he falls in love with Madalena.

The extraordinary fluidity of identity which structures the comedy, with guises being adopted as and when necessary or desired, finds its ultimate ingenious expression in the name 'Don Dionís' which, knowingly or not, is adopted by all four main protagonists:

(1) Mireno assumes the identity of Don Dionís, only to have that identity fortuitously confirmed at the close of the play by his father who, having been revealed not to be the shepherd

Lauro (an identity he adopted because of political intrigue against him) but the Duke of Coimbra, reveals in turn that his son's name actually *is* Don Dionís.

(2) Madalena plays the character Mireno / Don Dionís in her dream.

(3) Serafina believes her own portrait as a man to be a portrait of someone called Don Dionís; as well as falling in love with herself therefore, she indirectly and unwittingly assumes the identity of Don Dionís in so far as she is the actual figure in the portrait.

(4) Antonio, Serafina's suitor, pretends to be the man in the portrait, Don Dionís. He thereby gives the notion of identity a further twist by pretending to be Don Dionís who, in so far as this Don Dionís is the 'man' in the portrait, is actually Serafina. Following this 'logic', he pretends therefore to be Serafina.

Using the name Don Dionís, Tirso presents the audience with a dizzying array of changes, twists, deceptions, and possibilities. He certainly does seem to present identity as performative, that is to say, he seems to present identity as a role which we select and which we choose to perform, rather than as something innate and fixed within us. This said, we must offset this decidedly modern idea with the fact that Tirso, following convention, has Mireno select unerringly what will eventually be confirmed as his true and proper identity, that the Don Dionís, a nobleman.

Just as in Lope's *Peribáñez*, then, we encounter a tension between a radical intimation concerning identity and a conservative resolution, with a character constructing an identity possessing qualities denied him by social stereotypes, only to have those qualities confirmed as innate. Whether or not Tirso is being ironic in his presentation of the cliché of innate nobility, he certainly does show how performance is an integral part of life and of identity, a source of comedy in the play, and also a means of working within and against social constraints.

Cross-dressing, as exemplified here by Rosaura (*La vida es sueño*) and Serafina (*El vergonzoso en palacio*), and role-play (by Serafina, Madalena, Mireno and Antonio) were frequent elements on the stage. Sometimes cross-dressing is merely titillating, especially in the rare instances when a male character dresses as a woman, but it also enables, however briefly and however unbelievably, rigid social codes to be transgressed and other possibilities to emerge. It is a way for women in particular to access greater freedom of action, movement and expression, and to challenge established social and religious norms.

2. Court

So far I have considered how the Baroque placed great emphasis on the notion of performance, of identity as projected and indeed constituted by its public role. In this way, a sense of self is formed primarily by the individual's social environment and by his or her social function. Thus Gutierre and Mencía, the protagonists in *El médico de su honra*, are defined predominantly by their social and marital status (a gentleman and a lady, a husband and a wife) rather than by their innate characteristics as unique individuals; indeed, it is these roles that create the tensions which the honour-driven plot unfolds.

When we turn from fiction to non-fiction, we find the same emphasis on the functional and performative projection of self prevailing, with image mattering more than reality. During this period many non-fictional works were written with the express aim of fashioning an individual. Such manuals followed the example of Baldassare Castiglione's hugely influential *Il cortegiano* (1528) in so far as their aim was to teach social graces and socially useful skills and so form the perfect gentleman.

Works such as Antonio López de Vega's *El perfecto señor, sueño político* (1626), Lorenzo de Guzmán's *Espejo de discretos* (1643), Gracián's series of handbooks – *El héroe, El discreto*, the *Oráculo manual* -, Francisco Gutiérrez de los Ríos' *El hombre práctico*, and Francisco Garau's *El sabio instruido de la naturaleza* (1691) endeavoured to teach the individual how to acquire an effective public persona premised on the ability to behave, react and perceive both as a *discreto* and as a gentleman. Some writers like Gracián suggested that discretion and prudence were the prerogative of the social elite. Others were less socially restrictive, holding out the possibility that anyone with a mind to do so could better themselves. The social aspirations and anxieties which many such manuals exploit had long been the butt of humour in picaresque fiction: Quevedo's *El buscón*, for example, adopts a deeply conservative stance towards any desire for social improvement and hence social mobility: the attempts of Pablos to construct and project a better persona fail spectacularly to his great humiliation. Furthermore, these works were almost entirely directed at men. Handbooks aimed at women tended to teach their readers to cultivate domestic rather than social skills so that they would make good Christian wives.

Connected with manuals of gentlemanly conduct were those works aimed at fashioning the individual to fulfil more specific roles, the favourite subject being the king himself. Representative titles include Francisco Bermúdez de Pedraza's *El secretario del rey* (1620), Juan Antonio de Vera y Figueroa's *El embajador* (1620), Quevedo's *Política de Dios, gobierno de Cristo*, Gracián's *El político*, Cristóbal de Benavente y Benavides' *Advertencias para reyes, príncipes y embajadores* (1643), Diego Enríquez de Villegas' *El príncipe en la idea* (1656), Andrés Mendo's *Príncipe perfecto y ministros ajustados*, and Antonio de Vieyra's *Aprovechar deleitando: Nueva idea de púlpito cristiano-político* (1660).

Such works were written throughout the century and were far more politically focused than those works which derived from the example of Castiglione. This political focus was frequently combined with an explicit Christian agenda, as can be seen from some of the titles themselves. All these manuals centre, in one way or another, on the Court as the key political institution of the country and act in part as guidebooks as to how the institution and its key players operated.

They are both descriptive and prescriptive at the same time, teaching the individual how to mould his behaviour to fit the institution and, using this didactic formula, often pass comment on Spain's political situation in a period of gradually waning power and authority. The vast majority of these treatises are now little studied, but in the Baroque they were extremely widely read. Though the combination of morality and politics often fails to rise above mere cliché, the best of these works grapple with many of the major political, social, moral and intellectual issues of the day – in prose which is as beautiful and crafted as that found in any contemporary fiction.

The pinnacle of this tradition is Diego de Saavedra Fajardo's *Idea de un príncipe político-cristiano*. This work is one of the greatest pieces of prose written in the Baroque and in its themes, style and tactics it epitomizes the entire period. By 1700 it had been translated into French, Dutch, German, Italian, English and Latin. Saavedra was an experienced diplomat and had worked at courts, and represented Spain in international treaty negotiations, in Italy, Germany and Switzerland. Via his work we gain a remarkably frank insight into one man's experience of the religious and political turmoils of Europe during the Thirty Years War.

As the title makes clear, Saavedra aims to combine political instruction with Christian precepts. The work is dedicated to Philip IV's son, Baltasar Carlos (1629-46), and attempts to educate the prince via a hundred *empresas*, each of which is followed by an essay which explores, extends and enforces the message conveyed by the *empresa*. He dissects the state and considers it from every conceivable angle, examining in the process the nature of Spain's decline and pinpointing three aspects on which success or failure depends: God, chance, and prudence (59). He returns to these three time and again across the treatise, and together with the notion of constancy (which, with prudence, was a political virtue much extolled by the Neostoics) they form the coordinates of Saavedra's political philosophy.

Whilst ostensibly concerned with the formation of the king's

character and public persona, Saavedra thus engages in an analysis
of many questions of contemporary political theory and practice.
This is because the king ultimately projects himself in and through
the state. In a sense, the state *is* the king's public persona (see 31
and 33). For the king, the personal is always political, and vice
versa. Consequently, in considering the image of the king within
Saavedra's work we also need necessarily to engage with his discussions of political issues. These discussions confront the challenges
posed by the decline in Spain's political fortunes, and the reper-
cussions of these for king and country, as well as those occasioned
by the culture of uncertainty, for, as I mentioned in Chapter Two,
Saavedra was favourably inclined towards scepticism. In so doing,
the *Idea* provides a considered picture of Baroque Spain by one of
its most engaging thinkers.

The *empresa*, often wrongly referred to as an emblem (with
which it has many similarities) was a pictorial representation or
device designed to symbolize an idea. Juan de Horozco y
Covarrubias gives a list of rules concerning *empresas* which help
define the genre. They include such things as that the *empresa* must
be accompanied by a brief, epigrammatic motto, that it depict no
human figure (the preserve of the emblem), that it not be based
on real events and past occurrences, and that 'no sea tan clara que
cualquiera la entienda, ni tan oscura que sea menester quien la
declare' (*Emblemas morales* [1589]: 'it must be neither so transparent that anyone can understand it, nor so opaque that it
requires someone to explain it'). The distinction between emblem
and *empresa* was not totally clear cut, but Saavedra's use of the term
largely conforms to Horozco's list of rules. Saavedra explains his
use of both the *empresa* and the essay by stating that this serves to
enforce the message, with the *empresa* itself encapsulating this in an
easily memorable way:

Propongo a V.A. la *Idea de un Príncipe Político-Cristiano*, representada
con el buril y con la pluma, para que por los ojos y por los oídos
(instrumentos del saber) quede más informado el ánimo de V.A. en

la ciencia de reinar, y sirvan las figuras de memoria artificiosa.
(Dedication)

(I offer Your Highness this *Idea*, depicted with both the engraver's
chisel and the writer's pen, so that through your eyes and ears (the
instruments of knowledge) your Highness' mind may be more
informed concerning the science of ruling, and so that the illustrations may serve as a form of memory aid.)

Echoing the ideas of art theorists, Saavedra thus uses the senses to
implant his moral and political lessons in the mind of the reader.
Furthermore, just as with the allegorical mode of Gracián's *El
Criticón*, the reader must delve beneath the visual appearance of
the *impresa* in order to penetrate its real meaning. The combination of pictorial device and political essay proved very popular in
Spain and was emulated by a number of writers in works written in
both Latin and Spanish such as Juan de Solórzano Pereira's
Emblemata regio-politica (1653), Mendo's *Príncipe perfecto*, and Juan
Baños de Velasco y Acebedo's *L. Anneo Séneca, ilustrado en blasones
políticos y morales* (1670).

The *empresa* and its accompanying essay tend to pull in different
directions, for whereas the *empresa* is general, ahistorical, visual
and elusive (one has to ponder its meaning), the essay which
expounds its content is specific, historically focused, discursive
and explicit. *Empresa* 50, for example, shows a large mountain
pointing towards the heavens with the motto 'Iovi et Fulmini'
('Close to Jupiter and his thunder' – see Illustration 2). The general idea is then briefly explained in the opening lines of the essay:
the closer one is to power (the king) the nearer one is both to his
favour and his displeasure. This is then applied to the *valimiento*,
the institution, begun by Philip III, of delegating power to a
favourite. Saavedra pursues his ideas on this contentious institution with examples drawn from Roman history, the Bible, and
contemporary events – mentioning, for example, the Duke of
Buckingham (James VI/I's favourite) and the Duke of Lerma
(Philip III's), but discretely refraining from dwelling on the Count-

Illustration 2

Diego de Saavedra Fajardo, *Idea de un príncipe político-cristiano*
(Empresa 50)

Duke of Olivares whose hold on power in the early 1640s was rapidly loosening. Such references to contemporary Europe are what gives the work its distinctive sense of hands-on engagement with real political issues and problems.

Whilst the entire work is concerned with the formation of the ideal prince, the second essay explicitly addresses the role of education in forming an individual. The *empresa* shows a blank canvas and a hand holding a palette and brushes. What this represents is the idea derived from Aristotle that our mind is at birth a blank tablet, a *tabula rasa*, waiting to be filled by experience.* Addressing this issue, Saavedra looks at the prince's early environment and underlines its importance by stating how potentially dangerous the court is, filled as it is with liars, flatterers and all manner of temptations. (His warnings here recall some of the plots of Calderón's court dramas mentioned in Chapter One.)

The importance of environment is fairly deterministic, for Saavedra also subscribes to the idea that individual temperaments are largely determined by the country and people into whom one is born, for he believes that geographical location and climate all affect the type of person one is (81). However, Saavedra echoes Calderón's orthodox line in *La vida es sueño* in stating that our environment only predisposes us to behave in certain ways and cannot compel us. Despite such a disclaimer, however, the overwhelming impression is that people are indeed determined by their environment. After all, Saavedra's aim in going through the various nations and climatic zones is precisely to teach the prince how best to deal with their inhabitants by informing him beforehand what they are like.

Saavedra presents politics and, more particularly, the prince's role, from a number of perspectives simultaneously. These reveal how for the king the personal and the political, the private and the

* This was a cliché and the image depicted in the *empresa* was a recurrent one in Baroque art – it occurs in Vicente Carducho's *Diálogos de la pintura*, for example, as well as in a painting by Valdés Leal entitled the *Allegory of Vanity*.

public, are necessarily always connected. For convenience's sake, these perspectives can be categorized into four interdependent positions: (1) the eternal perspective; (2) the historical or human perspective; (3) the political or international perspective; and (4) the pragmatic perspective.

(1) *The eternal perspective.* This is the primary perspective – the prince must constantly remember God's imperatives in all his words and deeds. The ultimate judge of his actions will be God, and God is the source of all the prince's temporal power: 'La mayor potestad desciende de Dios. Antes que en la tierra, se coronaron los reyes en su eterna mente' (18: 'The greatest power comes from God. Before they were crowned on earth, kings were crowned in God's eternal mind').

(2) *The historical perspective.* The prince needs constantly to measure his actions against the past, considering carefully both his ancestors and other rulers, and learning from their example whether positive and negative. He needs also to think of the future, both in terms of how posterity will judge him and how his own actions will help or hinder his successors. This perspective gives the work its strong sense of temporal continuity, the prince being taught to view himself as one element on the continuum of past, present, and future. To enforce the point, Saavedra often draws on the notion of equality in the eyes of God, making the prince realize that his position and power are temporary, kingship a mere role allotted to him to perform:

> Muchas cosas hacen común al príncipe con los demás hombres, y una sola, y ésa accidental, le diferencia . . . Piense que es hombre y que gobierna hombres. Considere bien que en el teatro del mundo sale a representar un príncipe, y que en haciendo su papel entrará otro con la púrpura que dejar; y de ambos solamente quedará después la memoria de haber sido. Tenga entendido que aun esa púrpura no es suya, sino de la república, que se la presta para que represente ser cabeza de ella[.] (19)

(Many things serve to make the prince like other men, and only one incidental thing differentiates him from them. . . . Let the prince then remember that he is human and that he is governing men. Let him ponder the fact that, in the theatre of the world, he enters the stage to play the role of a prince, but that once his role is done another will enter wearing the very royal robes he has left behind. And eventually all that will remain of both will be a mere memory. Let him bear in mind that his royal trappings belong not to him but to the people who lend them to him so that he can act the role of their leader.)

The work's emphasis on past, present and future arises in part from the notion of prudence which has a central role within the treatise, for prudence is the political virtue which, as Saavedra comments following Cicero, operates on a temporal span: 'consta esta virtud de la prudencia de muchas partes, las cuales se reducen a tres: memoria de lo pasado, inteligencia de lo presente y providencia de lo futuro' (28: 'the virtue prudence has many aspects which can be reduced to three: memory of what is past, understanding of what is present, and foresight concerning what is to come').

(3) *The political perspective.* An accurate and detailed knowledge of events in the national and international arenas, as well as general knowledge of how to govern (based on an awareness of human nature which will teach the prince how to handle subordinates and subjects successfully), are presented as an absolute necessity. Paraphrasing the Bible (*Ecclesiastes* 1,9), Saavedra claims, in a rare optimistic moment, that such knowledge will enable infallible knowledge of the future to be gained: 'conocidos bien estos dos tiempos, pasado y presente, conocerá también V.A. el futuro; porque ninguna cosa nueva debajo del sol. Lo que es, fue; y lo que fue, será. Múdanse las personas, no las escenas' (28: 'if these two aspects, past and present, are known, then Your Highness will also know the future, for there is nothing new under the sun. What is, was. And what was, will be again. People come and go, but not the

scenes and situations which they find themselves in'.) This idea
derives from Tacitus, and is found in writers as diverse as Alamos
de Barrientos and Vera y Figueroa.

(4) *The pragmatic perspective.* Saavedra is no idealist. He realizes that
the prince is human and fallible, that he is as capable of being
deceived as anyone, and that his position and power mean that he
is especially vulnerable to flattery and lies. The prince is thus
taught not to expect perfection, to learn how to compromise, and
to do the best he can, however far that falls short of the ideal: 'No
ha de ser el gobierno como debiera, sino como puede ser; porque
no todo lo que fuera conveniente es posible a la fragilidad
humana' (85: 'The government does not have to be as it should
ideally be, but rather as best it can be, for not everything which is
advantageous is possible for human frailty'). Above all, the ruler
must be flexible in his attitudes, behaviour and way of doing
things, for only in this way will he dominate circumstances (36). In
this way Saavedra teaches that rules rigidly followed are as likely to
lead astray as they are to help. An ability to change with the times
is the surest route to success.

Engaging with contemporary debates concerning scepticism,
Saavedra's pragmatism comes across forcibly in his advice concerning deception and its perception (43-48). We see this clearly in
his advice concerning deceit. This was an area of debate which
greatly absorbed historians and writers on political theory since it
concerned the vexed questions of whether the means can justify
the end and whether the prince should simply appear to be virtuous and above reproach or whether he really should possess
virtue absolutely.

Regarding the latter point Saavedra devotes an entire essay to
the refutation of Machiavelli's ideas which he summarizes as follows:

No le parece que las virtudes son necesarias en él, sino que basta el
dar a entender que las tiene; porque, si fuesen verdaderas y siempre

se gobernase por ellas, le serían perniciosas, y al contrario, fructuosas si se pensase que las tenía. (18)

(He thinks that virtue is unnecessary for the prince, and that he must simply give out that he possesses it; arguing that if he truly possessed virtue and always ruled following its dictates, then virtue would cause him great harm, whereas to be perceived to have virtue will bring great benefit.)

His idealism in opposing such opportunism is not without an opportunistic streak itself, however. For he freely suggests that pursuing virtue will bring its own political rewards: 'la virtud tiene fuerza para atraer a Dios a nuestros intentos, no la malicia' ('virtue has the force to attract God over to our ventures, but not malice').

When he later turns to ponder whether the prince himself should use deceit, Saavedra moves away from the influential position of Justus Lipsius who had distinguished three levels of deceit: 'light deceit' (dissimulation, such as concealing the truth, permissable because we live in a deceitful world and the prince will get nowhere if he refuses to fight like with like); 'middle deceit' (purchasing favour and active deception, to be used sparingly); and 'great deceit' (treachery and injustice – sinful and to be avoided).

Of Lipsius' thinking, Saavedra says:

Si es vicioso el engaño, vicioso será en sus partes, por pequeñas que sean, y indigno del príncipe. No sufre mancha alguna lo precioso de la púrpura real. No hay átomo tan sutil, que no se descubra y afee los rayos de estos soles de la tierra. . . . No puede haber engaño que no se componga de la malicia y de la mentira, y ambas son opuestas a la magnanimidad real. . . . Lo que es ilícito nunca se debe permitir, ni basta sea el fin honesto para usar de un medio por su naturaleza malo. Solamente puede ser lícita la disimulación y astucia cuando ni engañan ni dejan manchado el crédito del príncipe. (43)

(If deceit is sinful, then even its smallest parts will be sinful and unworthy of the prince. The priceless royal robes can suffer not the slightest stain, and even the smallest atom is visible and will blemish these terrestrial suns. . . . There is no deceit which does not involve malice and lies, and both are the very opposite of royal magnanimity . . . What is illicit should never be allowed, nor is it sufficient to have a decent end in sight to justify the use of a means which is by its very nature bad. Dissimulation and cunning are only permissible when they neither deceive nor stain the prince's reputation.)

What is interesting here is that, for all his rejection of the idea of the end justifying the means, Saavedra's reasoning against Lipsius enables him nevertheless to arrive at the same conclusion – that dissimulation is permissable.

Significantly this reasoning is based on the Spanish obsession with honour and reputation, for he advocates that the acceptability of *engaño* should be measured according to the effects it will have on a prince's reputation and honour. The images used concerning the stain on the prince's robe and the sun recall Calderón's wife-murder plays in which, as we have seen, the mere appearance of a blot on the husband's honour is sufficient to compel him to commit murder.

In an essay on the importance of reputation to the state's image he again presents the concept in terms reminiscent of the theatre – 'Un acto solo derriba la reputación, y muchos no la pueden restaurar, porque no hay mancha que se limpie sin dejar señales, ni opinión que se borre enteramente' (31: 'A single act topples reputation, and many acts cannot restore it for there is no stain which can be cleaned up without leaving a mark and no opinion which can be removed completely').

Like Gracián, then, Saavedra is a pragmatist, recognizing that it is appearances more than reality which count most in maintaining a state: 'No hay monarquía tan poderosa, que no la sustente más la opinión que la verdad' (81: 'There is no monarchy so powerful that it is not maintained more by opinion than truth'). It is for this reason that the king needs to be both a visible and a distant figure: he needs to be seen to be powerful, virtuous etc., but to maintain the mystique of majesty, he also needs to keep his distance so that his image can remain untainted by the perception of any flaws.

Combining these four perspectives, the work attempts to cover every aspect of experience, moving, like Gracián's *El Criticón*, through the stages of a prince's life, from birth to death. Saavedra's objective is the objective of all such manuals – to help the individual play the role allotted to him to the best of his abilities. The nature of the prince's role as essentially a performance for purposes of state comes across most strongly in the *Idea*'s emphasis on visibility. This is conveyed via several metaphors among which is the clock (57). According to this metaphor the prince is the visible manifestation of monarchy (the clock's hands) while his ministers (the wheels and cogs) work behind the scenes to maintain the state. It is precisely this very visibility which makes it so imperative that the prince be seen to be as perfect an embodiment of the ideal ruler as possible.

A king is both a human being and, as the monarch, the symbolic embodiment of a state. Saavedra attempts to bridge the gulf between these two potentially conflictive positions by teaching how the particular quirks, desires and personal characteristics of the individual must be subordinated to the demands of his role as king – this is largely the subject of the work's second section (7-37).

Nowhere do we see so clearly how the individual is formed by his or her social role and function, nor how strongly the individual is coerced by the sense of social duty. Saavedra is acutely aware that for Baltasar Carlos, his nominal addressee, the situation of Spain on the world stage was critical and that there was only so much that any ruler could do to reverse what he saw as an inevitable decline. Of course, by viewing decline as inevitable he attempts to offer some comfort by thereby portraying it as natural ('Tienen su período los imperios. El que más duró, más cerca está de su fin': 'All empires have an allotted period. The one which has lasted longest is the one which is nearest to its end' [87]).

In a similar, somewhat half-hearted, way he encourages the prince – and his readers – not to be fatalistic in the face of certain decline, commenting that 'no podemos romper aquella tela de los sucesos, tejida en los telares de la eternidad, pero pudimos concurrir a tejerla' (88: 'we cannot tear the cloth of events woven in eternity's workshop, but we could have actively joined in its weaving'). Despite such comments, the prince, the favourite, the courtier, the gentleman, however successfully they play their roles, are all fated by history to appear in a second-rate production, and to be judged accordingly:

> Infelices los sujetos grandes que nacen en las monarquías cadentes; porque, o no son empleados, o no pueden resistir el peso de sus ruinas, y envueltos en ellas, caen miserablemente sin crédito ni opinión, y a veces parecen culpados en aquello que forzosamente había de suceder. (87)

> (How unfortunate are those noble individuals who are born into monarchies which are declining. Either they are never employed, or they are unable to resist the weight of the collapsing monarchies and, crushed by them, they fall pitiably having gained neither credit nor opinion, and sometimes they are even blamed for what had inevitably to happen.)

In this truly pessimistic and, one feels, heart-felt comment, Saavedra expresses the king's predicament: the tension and conflict between the individual and his or her environment, the desires of the former being inevitably limited and curtailed by the pressures of the latter.

To put this in the terms examined so relentlessly by Cervantes, Saavedra and his contemporaries were faced with a conflict between idealism and reality. Idealism posits a ruler who never lies or dissembles, and a Spain which is dominant, devout and victorious. But reality compromises such ideal aspirations as we have seen. Just as the general, abstract message of each *empresa* is particularized by the historical and political contextualization in its accompanying essay, so similarly ideals are compromised when they come into contact with a particular historical context: the reality in which Philip IV, Baltasar Carlos, the Count-Duke of Olivares and Saavedra find themselves. Consequently, for all his emphasis on the performance of the king as vital to Spain's image, and on the political success of Spain as vital to the king's image, comments such as the ones I have just mentioned reveal that Saavedra is more than aware that the trappings of power can do little in reality to reverse the inevitable. The illusion of authority and power is no substitute for the real thing, and for all the importance of image and reputation for both king and state, if reality is too far removed from appearances, then there is little that can be done to bridge this credibility gap. It is here, then, that we encounter most forcibly the disillusion that can result when a nation's self-image, the sense of identity it both desires and endeavours to project, fails to match reality. Indeed, the compulsive drive towards *desengaño* only serves to strip away the outer trappings of a once great power and reveal to the reader its inner emptiness.

Further reading:

Robert Bireley, *The Counter-Reformation Prince: Anti-Machiavellianism or Catholic Statecraft in Early Modern Europe* (Chapel Hill and London, 1990) – excellent chapter on Saavedra

Victor Dixon, *Caracterization in the comedia of Seventeenth-Century Spain* (Manchester, 1994)

José A. Fernández-Santamaría, *Reason of State and Statecraft in Spanish Political Thought, 1595-1640* (Lanham, New York and London, 1983) – excellent overview of a little studied area

Fernando R. de la Flor, *Lecturas de la imagen simbólica* (Madrid, 1995) – wide-ranging consideration of emblems etc. in Spanish culture

Melveena McKendrick, 'Calderón's Justina: The Assumption of Selfhood', in *Feminist Readings on Spanish and Latin-American Literature*, edited by L. Conde and S.M. Hart (Lewiston, New York, 1991)

José Maravall, *La teoría española del estado en el siglo XVII* (Madrid, 1944)
George Mariscal, *Contradictory Subjects: Quevedo, Cervantes, and Seventeenth-Century Spanish Culture* (Ithaca and London, 1991)
Jeremy Robbins, 'Male Dynamics in Calderón's *A secreto agravio, secreta venganza*', *Hispanófila*, 117 (1996), pp.11-24 – discusses the relationship between honour and male identity.

VII
Conclusion

Given the extraordinary diversity of the art and literature produced in the seventeenth century it is difficult to reach a single conclusion capable of encompassing its range and complexity. What I have tended to emphasize in this study are the ways in which Spanish culture was a response to a complex and changing intellectual and political milieu. The result of such complexity is that many works pull in two directions simultaneously.

This can be seen by citing just some of the examples mentioned over the course of the previous chapters which, in so many different ways, draw on the complex meanings and applications of the period's two omnipresent and intimately connected sets of terms, *ser* and *parecer*, *engaño* and *desengaño*: Murillo's and Valdés Leal's paintings for the Church of the Hospital de la Santa Caridad (temporal versus eternal, challenge versus comfort); Cervantes' *Don Quijote*, Velázquez's *Meninas* and Gracián's *El Criticón* (idealism versus realism, fact versus fiction, illusion versus reality); Góngora's *Polifemo* (order versus chaos, beauty versus ugliness); and Saavedra's *Idea* (visual versus intellectual, general versus specific).

In a similar way Baroque culture is striking for its dual nature as both a public and a private affair: the public consumption in theatres, academies, churches and palaces of art which nonetheless was supposed to invoke an intimate, private reaction and response; the love of dazzling spectacle, and the exhortations to inner meditation and reaction. It is such antithetical tensions which make Baroque art and literature so dynamic and alive. We see through them and in them a society struggling to express complexity and its own feelings, apprehensions, and excitement in the face of such complexity.

By emphasizing these antitheses at the heart of the Baroque I mean to highlight something more than that Baroque culture is more complex than it might at first appear, or that Baroque culture contains contradictory elements. Rather, the obsessive, indeed compulsive, way in which the Spanish Baroque expresses and explores the tension between *ser* and *parecer* in its art, theatre, prose and poetry is a direct result of what I have called the culture of doubt and uncertainty. For a variety of reasons (intellectual, political and religious) this culture of uncertainty constituted the environment in which seventeenth-century artists, poets, prose writers and dramatists worked.

Their unwillingness to move away from the simultaneous expression of opposites is the ultimate expression of such uncertainty, for it is indicative of a refusal, perhaps even an inability, to simplify, and of a concomitant desire to be inclusive in the face of opposing impulses, ideas, and possibilities. It is also, of course, a way of shifting moral and interpretative responsibility onto individuals who are thus made to reflect for themselves upon the complex question of the nature of the human engagement with reality that so many Baroque works relentlessly explore. It is this challenge to the individual which makes it still so attractive and compelling, engaging our senses and our minds in the task of encountering another culture.

Glossary

Alamos de Barrientos, Baltasar (1555-1640s): political theorist, influential in propagating the ideas of Tacitus in his *Tácito español ilustrado con Aforismos* (1614)

Alemán, Mateo (1547-1615): author of the widely-read picaresque novel *Guzmán de Alfarache* (1599 and 1604)

Arguijo, Juan de (1567-1623): poet, active in literary circles in Seville

Bances Candamo, Francisco (1662-1704): playwright and author of last major treatise on the theatre, the *Teatro de los teatros* (1689-94)

Baños de Velasco y Acevedo, Juan (1615-82): historian and author of works of moral and political philosophy, influenced by Stoicism

Barrionuevo de Peralta, Jerónimo de (1587-1671): author of a series of news letters (1654-58) chronicling life in Madrid

Benavente y Benavides, Cristóbal de (1582-1650s?): courtier and ambassador, author of *Advertencias para reyes, príncipes y embajadores* (1643)

Bermúdez de Pedraza, Francisco (1585-1655): jurist and historian

Bianco, Baccio del (1604-57): Italian scene designer, employed by Philip IV from 1651 to design court plays after the death in 1643 of the previous Italian scenographer Cosimo Lotti who had worked in Spain since 1626

Bocángel y Unzueta, Gabriel (1603-58): important poet, active in literary academies, librarian to Philip IV's brother, the Cardenal-Infante

Calderón de la Barca, Pedro (1600-81): one of Spain's greatest playwrights, composing mythological court dramas and *autos sacramentales*, for which he enjoyed a virtual monopoly in Madrid, and many comedies, tragedies and religious plays for the commercial stage, an activity he abandoned in 1651 when he was ordained

Cáncer y Velasco, Jerónimo de (1594-1654): poet, satirist, and playwright, active in Madrid academies

Cano, Alonso (1601-67): artist and sculptor, renowned for his virulent anti-semitism

Caramuel y Lobkowitz, Juan (1606-82): Cistercian, and a Cartesian intellectual polymath

Carducho, Vicente (c1576-1638): court artist, rival of Velázquez, and author of the *Diálogos de la pintura* (1633)

Caro Mallén de Soto, Ana (c1600-1650s): playwright and poet, best known for her play *Valor, agravio y mujer*

Carreño de Miranda, Juan (1614-85): major court artist, representative of late Baroque style; (see *Rizi*)

Carrillo y Sotomayor, Luis (1581/82-1610): poet and theorist, composed the *Fábula de Acis y Galatea*; in his *Libro de la erudición poética* (1611) advocated, like Góngora, a deliberately difficult poetic style

Carvajal y Saavedra, Mariana de (1610/15-c1665): author of collection of short stories, the *Navidades de Madrid y noches entretenidas* (1663)

Cascales, Francisco (1564-1642): polemicist in the debate over Góngora's innovations, taking a conservative line in his *Tablas poéticas* (1617) and the *Cartas filológicas* (1634)

Castillo Solórzano, Alonso de (1584-1648?): dramatist, novelist and academy poet

Castro, Guillén de (1569-1631): dramatist on whose best-known work, *Las mocedades del Cid*, Corneille based *Le Cid*

Cervantes Saavedra, Miguel de (1547-1616): Spain's greatest novelist, author of *Don Quijote* (1605, 1615), as well as of a pastoral novel *La Galatea* (1585) and a Byzantine romance *Los trabajos de Persiles y Sigismunda* (1617); also wrote the *Novelas ejemplares* (1613), as well as various pieces for the theatre

Charles II (1661-1700): son of Philip IV and Mariana of Austria, King of Spain, reigned 1665-1700

Coello, Claudio (early 1640s-93): court artist and architect, his most famous painting is the *trompe l'oeil La sagrada forma* in the Escorial

Corral, Gabriel de (1588-late 1640s): novelist, poet, and academy veteran

Cubillo de Aragón, Alvaro (1596?-1661): playwright and poet, active in literary life and academies in Madrid

Enríquez Gómez, Antonio (1600-63): dramatist, poet, and author of the picaresque-like work *El siglo pitagórico* (1644); fled Spain to France; and burnt in effigy by the Inquisition for his Judaism, eventually dying in prison in Spain

Enríquez de Villegas, Diego (dates unknown): Portuguese historian and political theorist

Espinosa Medrano, Juan de (1640?-88): Peruvian writer and dramatist, author of an important defence of Góngora

Esquilache, Prince of (1581-1658): major political figure, viceroy of Peru, and important poet

Faria y Sousa, Manuel de (1590-1649): Portuguese poet active in literary circles and academies in Madrid, anti-Góngora's innovations

Garau, Francisco (1640-1701): Jesuit, moral philosopher

Góngora y Argote, Luis de (1561-1627): the greatest poet of the Spanish Baroque, his *Polifemo* and *Soledades* giving rise to a vigorous literary debate and exercising an enormous influence on fellow poets; wrote many sonnets, ballads and satirical poems

Gracián, Baltasar (1601-58): Jesuit, author of various moral and political treatises, and *El criticón* (1651-57); his works influenced various European writers; wrote under a patently obvious pseudonym supposedly to side-step the criticism of his Jesuit superiors

Gutiérrez de los Ríos, Francisco, Count of Fernán Núñez (1644-1717): courtier, and author of *El hombre práctico* (1686), often taken to be a forerunner of the Spanish Enlightenment

Guzmán, Fray Lorenzo de (?-1651): theologian and moral philosopher

Haro, Luis de (1598-1661): principal minister of Philip IV after the fall of Olivares

Herrera y Tordesillas, Antonio de (1549-1626): historian and translator, promoter of Tacitus

Herrera, Francisco, the Elder (1589/91-1654/57): artist and architect, trained by Pacheco

Herrera, Francisco, the Younger (1627-85): son of the above, court artist and chief court architect

Hurtado de Mendoza, Antonio (1586-1644): major court poet under Philip IV, writing plays for, and eulogistic verse about, the court

Isabel of Bourbon (1603-44): first wife of Philip IV, mother of Baltasar Carlos (1629-46)

Jáuregui, Juan de (1583-1641): artist, poet, translator, and literary theorist, a major figure in the anti-Góngora camp

Juan José of Austria (1629-79): bastard son of Philip IV, a major focus of opposition to the regency of Mariana of Austria

Juana Inés de la Cruz, Sor (1648-95): Mexican nun, dramatist, poet, and author of one of the first serious feminist treatises, the *Respuesta a Sor Filotea de la Cruz* (1691)

Lerma, Duke of (1553-1625): favourite of Philip III until his fall in 1618

López Pinciano, Alonso (c1545-?): author of the influential literary treatise *Filosofía antigua poética* (1596)

López de Úbeda, Francisco (c1545-?): author of the picaresque novel *La pícara Justina* (1605)

López de Vega, Antonio (c1586-c1656): Portuguese writer and poet, remarkable for his independence of thought

López de Zárate, Francisco (1580-1658): love poet and writer of outstanding moral poetry

Lucio Espinosa y Malo, Félix de (1646-91): minor poet and prose writer of works like the *Epístolas varias* (1675)

Maino, Fray Juan Bautista (1578-1641): artist and drawing instructor to Philip IV

Mañara, Miguel de (1627-79): head of the Hermandad de la Santa Caridad, Seville, and author of the *Discurso de la verdad* (1679)

Marcela de San Félix, Sor (1605-97): illegitimate daughter of Lope de Vega, poet and dramatist, though unpublished in her own life

María de Jesús de Agreda, Sor (1602-65): confidant of Philip IV, author of the *Mística ciudad de Dios*, and a mystic who claimed to be able to be in two places at once

Mariana of Austria (1634-96): second wife of Philip IV; queen regent on his death in 1665

Martínez Montañés, Juan (1568-1649): one of the century's most famous sculptors

Mazo, Juan Bautista Martínez (1610/12-67): court artist, trained by Velázquez, his father-in-law

Méndez Silva, Rodrigo (1607-70s): historian, genealogist, and a moralist much influenced by Quevedo

Mendo, Andrés (1608-84): Jesuit, author of works of popular moral philosophy, influenced by Solórzano Pereira

Mira de Amescua, Antonio (1574?-1644): playwright, author of *El esclavo del demonio*

Moreto y Cabaña, Agustín (1618-69): dramatist, best known for his comedy *El desdén con el desdén*

Murillo, Bartolomé Esteban (1618-82): one of the Baroque's greatest artists, renowned for his depictions of the Immaculate Conception and religious subjects

Nieremberg, Juan Eusebio (1595-1658): Jesuit, author of *Curiosa filosofía* (1630), a work of pseudo-science, and *De la diferencia entre lo temporal y lo eterno* (1640)

Olivares, Count-Duke of (1587-1645): favourite of Philip IV from 1621-43; major source of patronage (e.g. Quevedo, Velázquez), initiating the rebuilding and expansion of the Buen Retiro palace

Pacheco, Francisco (1564-1644): artist, master of, and father-in-law to, Velázquez, and author of the *Arte de la pintura* (1649)

Palomino, Acisclo Antonio (1655-1726): court artist and author of *El museo pictórico y escala óptica* (1715, 1724)

Paravicino, Fray Hortensio Félix (1580-1633): orator and poet, famed for his style as a court preacher

Pellicer y Tovar, José de (1602-79): major figure in the literary life of Madrid; poet, genealogist, and eulogist of the Court

Pereda, Antonio de (1611-78): artist, probable painter of one of the century's most famous works, the *Dream of the Knight*

Pérez de Montalbán, Juan (1602-38): novelist and playwright, his *Para todos* (1633) provides numerous details on fellow writers

Philip III (1578-1621): son of Philip II and Anne of Austria, King of Spain, reigned 1598-1621; instituted the *valimiento*, the delegation of authority to a favourite

Philip IV (1605-65): son of Philip III and Margarita of Austria, King of Spain, reigned 1621-65

Quevedo y Villegas, Francisco de (1580-1645): prolific writer, one of the greatest love poets in Spanish, and a hugely influential satirist; author of *El buscón*, the *Sueños*, and many works of moral philosophy heavily indebted to Neostoic thought; major rival of Góngora's

Ribadeneira, Pedro de (1526-1611): Jesuit, author of works of history, devotion, and political theory

Ribalta, Francisco (1564-1628): artist active in Valencia

Ribera, Anastasio Pantaleón de (1600-29): satirical poet and major academy figure in Madrid

Ribera, José de (1591-1652): one of the greatest Baroque artists, spent his working life in Naples developing a graphically realistic style influenced by Caravaggio

Rioja, Francisco de (1583-1659): poet, librarian to Philip IV

Rizi, Francisco (1614-85): major court artist, trained by Vicente Carducho, and representative of late Baroque theatrical style; painted the dome of San Antonio de los Alemanes in Madrid with Carreño, one of the few major Baroque frescos to survive; designed sets for the court theatres in Madrid

Rojas Zorrilla, Francisco de (1607-48): dramatist and poet, active in academies, famed for his tragedies

Roldán, Luisa (c1654-c1704): sculptor, daughter of Pedro Roldán

Roldán, Pedro (1624-99): important sculptor; worked on the altar of the church of the Hermandad de la Santa Caridad

Ruiz de Alarcón, Juan (1580-1639): Mexican born dramatist active in Madrid, butt of vicious satirical poems by fellow writers, author of the comedy *La verdad sospechosa*

Saavedra Fajardo, Diego de (1584-1648): diplomat and important political theorist, author of various political, satirical and historical works

Salinas, Count of (1564-1630): major poet and important political figure, Viceroy of Portugal (1616-1621)

Sánchez, Francisco (1550-1623): Portuguese doctor, author of sceptical treatise *Quod nihil scitur* (1581)

Sánchez Cotán, Fray Juan (1560-1627): major artist, famous for his still-life paintings

Setanti, Joaquín (dates unknown): Catalan author of political maxims influenced by Tacitus

Sigüenza y Góngora, Carlos de (1645-1700): major Mexican intellectual, produced numerous writings on philosophical, astronomical, historical and religious subjects

Solís y Rivadeneira, Antonio de (1610-86): historian, poet and dramatist

Solórzano Pereira, Juan de (1575-1653/54): jurist, political theorist, author of *Emblemata regio-politica* (1653)

Soto de Rojas, Pedro (1584-1658): poet greatly influenced by Góngora, especially in his *Paraíso cerrado para muchos, jardines abiertos para pocos* (1652); active in academies

Suárez de Figueroa, Cristóbal (1571?-1644?): prose writer whose *El pasajero* (1617) offers an insight into contemporary society and literary issues

Tirso de Molina, pseudonym of Fray Gabriel Téllez (c1584-1648): one of the greatest playwrights of the Golden Age, probable author of *El burlador de Sevilla,* which introduced the figure of Don Juan into European culture and on which Molière based his *Dom Juan*; in 1625 was forbidden to write by the *Junta de Reformación* on the grounds that his plays depicted reprehensible behaviour and set bad examples

Torre y Sevil, Francisco de la (1625-c1680): important poet active in academy circles especially in Zaragoza and Valencia

Valdés Leal, Juan de (1622-90): one of the last great artists of the Golden Age, painted many religious subjects, most famous for his *vanitas* paintings

Valencia, Pedro de (1555-1620): humanist scholar, friend of Góngora, and major supporter of his poetic innovations

Van der Hamen y León, Juan (1596-1631): major artist famous for his still-life paintings

Vega Carpio, Lope de (1562-1635): the most prolific dramatist of the Golden Age, developing the distinctive form of the *comedia*; also a major lyric, epic, and burlesque poet, as well as a prose writer

Velázquez y Silva, Diego de (1599-1660): the greatest Spanish artist; trained in Seville by Pacheco; an official in the court of Philip IV; one of the few artists to paint mainly secular subjects

Vélez de Guevara, Luis (1579-1644): poet, dramatist, novelist and satirist, author of *El diablo cojuelo* (1641), active in court circles and academies

Vera y Figueroa, Juan Antonio de, Count of la Roca (1588-1658): close friend of Count-Duke of Olivares, ambassador, and author of the influential *El embajador* (1620)

Vieyra, Antonio de (1608-97): Portuguese Jesuit, renowned for his oratory; Sor Juana wrote a critique of one of his sermons

Villamediana, Count of (1582-1622): major poet, follower of Góngora with mythological poems such as the *Fábula de Faetón*; important figure in the courts of Philip III and IV; renowned for his barbed epigrams, he was murdered – some saying for his supposed affair with the queen, others for his purported homosexuality

Zabaleta, Juan de (c1610-c1670): playwright, prose writer, and moralist, his most famous works, *El día de fiesta por la mañana* (1654) and *El día de fiesta por la tarde* (1660), offering a detailed account of contemporary society at play

Zayas y Sotomayor, María de (1590-1660?): poet and feminist novelist

Zurbarán, Francisco de (1598-1664): major artist, best known for his

exquisite statuesque portraits of saints and members of religious
orders; commissioned to paint works for the Buen Retiro, but
spent most of his career in Seville

Index